It is easy to see, that it would require an uncommon portion of fortitude in the judges to do their duty as faithful guardians of the Constitution, where legislative invasions of it had been instigated by the major voice of the community.

Alexander Hamilton, *Federalist* No. 78

JUDICIAL FORTITUDE

The Last Chance to Rein in the Administrative State

Peter J. Wallison

Encounter
BOOKS

New York • London

First American edition published in 2018 by Encounter Books, an activity of Encounter for Culture and Education, Inc., a nonprofit, tax exempt corporation. Encounter Books website address: www.encounterbooks.com

Manufactured in the United States and printed on acid-free paper. The paper used in this publication meets the minimum requirements of ANSI/NISO Z39.48-1992 (R 1997) (*Permanence of Paper*).

FIRST AMERICAN EDITION

LIBRARY OF CONGRESS CATALOGING-IN-PUBLICATION DATA

Names: Wallison, Peter J.
Title: Judicial fortitude : the last chance to rein in the administrative state / by Peter J. Wallison.
Description: New York : Encounter Books, 2018. |
Includes bibliographical references and index.
Identifiers: LCCN 2018011248 (print) | LCCN 2018012291 (ebook) |
ISBN 9781641770095 (ebook) | ISBN 9781641770088 (hardcover : alk. paper)
Subjects: LCSH: Judicial review of administrative acts—United States. |
Separation of powers—United States. |
United States—Politics and government.
Classification: LCC KF5425 (ebook) | LCC KF5425 .W35 2018 (print) |
DDC 347.73/12—dc23
LC record available at https://lccn.loc.gov/2018011248

Interior page design and composition: BooksByBruce.com

Dedication

To Justice Clarence Thomas, who has consistently seen the danger
to our Constitution in the erosion of the separation of powers. As he
wrote in 2015:

> We have too long abrogated our duty to enforce the separation of
> powers required by our Constitution. We have overseen and sanc-
> tioned the growth of an administrative system that concentrates
> the power to make laws and the power to enforce them in the
> hands of a vast and unaccountable administrative apparatus that
> finds no comfortable home in our constitutional structure. The
> end result may be trains that run on time (although I doubt it),
> but the cost is to our Constitution and the individual liberty
> it protects.

CONTENTS

INTRODUCTION

It is not too much to say that we risk losing our democracy unless we can gain control of the agencies of the administrative state. Rulemaking by unelected officials, with little congressional or judicial oversight, affects the lives of Americans in profound ways, but we have failed thus far to develop an effective strategy for controlling it. Congress has not been able to place limits on the growth of administrative power, and the courts have made the problem worse by requiring—in the 1984 decision *Chevron v. NRDC*—that lower courts defer to agencies' interpretations of their own statutory authorities. In this way, the judiciary has largely surrendered its constitutional duty to determine the scope of administrative discretion.

This is not the Framers' design. They structured a tripartite system of separated powers in which each branch of the government had an assigned but limited role. Congress was to be the exclusive source of legislation; the president was to execute the laws made by Congress; and the judiciary was to keep the elected branches—Congress and the president—within their designated areas of responsibility.

The Judiciary's Unique Role

In *Federalist* No. 78, Alexander Hamilton describes the crucial duty of the judiciary in the new constitutional system, and why—to properly fulfill that duty—judges must have life tenure:

> If…the courts of justice are to be considered as the bulwarks of a limited Constitution against legislative encroachments, this consideration will afford a strong argument for the *permanent tenure of judicial offices*, since nothing will contribute so much to this as that independent spirit in the judges, which must be essential to the

faithful performance of so arduous a duty…. But it is easy to see, that it would require an *uncommon portion of fortitude in the judges* to do their duty as faithful *guardians of the Constitution*, where legislative invasions of it had been instigated by the major voice of the community. (Emphasis added)[1]

The judiciary's position as the "guardians of the Constitution" received additional support from Chief Justice John Marshall in the foundational decision *Marbury v. Madison*, issued in 1803. There, he not only established that the Supreme Court could declare acts of Congress unconstitutional but also set out an equally important role for the judiciary: "It is emphatically the province and duty of the Judicial Department to say what the law is."[2]

These principles, as the Framers intended, placed the judiciary in a special position to decide the two issues essential to the separation of powers in the Constitution: first, whether Congress, in derogation of its exclusive constitutional role as legislator, has delegated its legislative power to the president or an agency of the executive branch; and, second, whether an administrative agency has exceeded the statutory authority it was granted by Congress.

Whether the result of timidity, adherence to precedent, or simply the difficulty of carrying out their unique role in the Framers' structure, the courts have largely failed to fulfill these responsibilities. And this—more than anything else—has contributed to the growth of the administrative state. In this book, I show not only that the Framers expected the judiciary to keep the other branches within their assigned roles, but also that the proper performance of that role is the only effective way to rein in the administrative state.

The separation of powers, outlined in chapter 2, is a unique feature of the U.S. Constitution. The Framers believed, from their study of history and political philosophy, that when the king (or any executive) controls the legislature or the courts—or when the legislature controls both the making and enforcing of the laws—the people's liberties are inevitably threatened. It is only when these three parts of a government—the legislature, the executive, and the judiciary—are kept independent of one another that liberty can be assured.

In 1787, after two years of debate by representatives from the original thirteen states, a draft constitution was submitted to the people for ratification. During the next two years, the Framers sought the public's support, which they finally won in 1788, when nine states had ratified.

Although protecting liberty was the Framers' stated objective, it was closely linked to the creation of a representative democracy. In the Framers' political theory, which followed John Locke's *Second Treatise of Government*,[3] the people—by ratifying the Constitution—transferred to the new government their inherent right to govern themselves. Congress, with the exclusive authority under the Constitution to make the laws, would be elected by and act on behalf of the people. Neither the president nor any administrative agency could act other than with the authority of the Constitution or a law enacted by Congress.

As shown in chapter 1, in many instances administrative agencies appear to have issued rules or interpreted their authority in ways that exceeded the powers they were given by Congress, but the courts have not intervened. Yet an administrative rule that exceeds the authority conferred by Congress is unconstitutional legislation, and when issued by an agency of the executive branch it represents exactly the combination of executive and legislative power that the Framers feared.

Checks and Balances

Although the Framers created a structure that gave the separate branches distinct powers, they also gave each of the branches some role in the functions of the others. The president, for example, participates in the legislative process through a power to veto legislation, and the courts can interpret the meaning and scope of the laws Congress enacts. Congress can impeach a president, refuse to fund presidential activities, and increase or decrease the number of judges on the federal courts.

Accordingly, the separation of powers should also be viewed as a system of checks and balances. The Framers saw this system—based on what they assumed would be a continuing interest of each of the three branches to protect its own authority—as assurance that the constitutional structure would not be easily overturned in the future. Each of the branches had the ability, to some degree, to hobble the other two if they stepped out of bounds. However, because of changes in the judiciary's perception of its role in this structure, together with major unanticipated changes in the role of Congress, described in chapter 3, this system is now in jeopardy.

The Progressive Drive for the Administrative State

The administrative state did not just spring into being because the United States grew larger between the Civil War and World War II. As discussed in chapter 4, the creation of powerful administrative agencies was largely the result of ideas developed during the Progressive Era, roughly between 1880 and 1920. The period was one of astounding economic growth and change, with unrestricted immigration, a great movement of population from rural areas to cities, the development of powerful corporate entities in oil, manufacturing, and finance, and the rise of railroads as a dominant feature of the transportation system.

Although the Framers saw the constitutional structure as necessary to protect liberty, reformers of the period—who styled themselves as Progressives—believed that structure was too conservative and slow-moving to deal with the country's serious new problems. Led by such major figures as Woodrow Wilson and Theodore Roosevelt, the Progressives saw the preservation of liberty as less important than creating a government with sufficient power and expertise to address society's new challenges. The speeches and writings of Wilson and Roosevelt made clear that both wanted to change the constitutional structure. Their objective was flexibility—a constitution that would change as the problems of the country and the needs of the American people changed—and they believed the Framers' Constitution was too rigid to meet that test. Wilson called the government a "living thing," anticipating today's concept of a "living Constitution."

The Progressive solution was to create agencies with specific responsibilities for regulating or supervising specialized sectors of the private economy so that they served the Progressives' idea of the "public interest." Traditional or conservative (we might call them classical liberal) forces resisted these changes, arguing that increasing government power would endanger liberty.

Thus was begun a historic contest between different approaches to the role of the government in the economy—a fight that, with the election of Woodrow Wilson in 1912, the Progressives won. Many powerful new agencies were established during the Progressive Era, and particularly the Wilson presidency. But after the First World War, and the election of Republican presidents Harding, Coolidge, and Hoover in the 1920s, it seemed as though the government might be returning to traditional constitutionalism. However, with the Great Depression, the election of Franklin D. Roosevelt, and the popularity of the New Deal, the themes and goals of the Progressive movement returned.

Early in FDR's tenure, the Supreme Court, led by Chief Justice Charles Evans Hughes, resisted some of the New Deal initiatives, striking down two laws in 1935 as unconstitutional delegations of legislative authority.[4] This is described in detail in chapter 6. However, Roosevelt's 1937 court-packing plan—even though it ultimately failed 70–20 in the Senate—appeared to cow the Court. Shortly after the plan was introduced, the Court—which had also declared some substantive New Deal legislation as violating a constitutional protection of contracts—seemed to reverse itself, with a 5–4 majority approving a state minimum-wage law. This gave rise to the popular idea that a "switch in time saved nine."[5] However, many subsequent Court retirements were far more important, allowing FDR to appoint seven new justices, all of whom had come of age during the Progressive Era. The decisions of these justices in later cases cemented Progressive views of government into the legal system. As Mark Tushnet observes:

> By the end of the 1930s [Justice] Frankfurter was in a position to write an opinion for the Court restating and endorsing the standard Progressive account of the rise of the administrative state and the Progressive vision of administrative procedure. In *FCC v. Pottsville Broadcasting Co.*, . . . the Court [ruled]: "Modern administrative tribunals . . . ha[d] been a response to the felt need of governmental supervision over economic enterprise—a supervision which could effectively be exercised neither directly, through self-executing legislation, nor by the judicial process."[6]

The combination of the Progressive ideas that dominated the New Deal, the profusion of government agencies created during this period, and the Supreme Court precedents established by the justices appointed in and after 1937 set the United States on a course that created today's administrative state.

Can Congress Rein in the Administrative State?

Chapter 6 discusses the nature of legislation, and the unique purpose and power of a legislature. In every society the question is always "Who decides?" There are many contending interests, and in a diverse republic such as the United States someone must make decisions that will inevitably please one group and disappoint others. That is the signal role of a legislature; as long as it stays within the confines of the constitutional structure, Congress (like any legislature) can be entirely arbitrary and discretionary in its choices and decisions, creating winners and losers without challenge. But legislating is difficult for just this reason, and there is a strong temptation for Congress to adopt laws that do not require a controversial decision. Too frequently, Congress has taken this easy route, leaving the difficult choices to administrative agencies.

If, for example, Congress authorizes an agency "to take all steps necessary to ensure that the waters of the United States are clean and healthful," few will object; but that is not a *legislative* decision, it is only the statement of a goal. The difficult questions come when the administrative agency has to implement the legislature's direction—who bears the costs, who gains or loses access to the water, and what waters are subject to government control? As the institution that is supposed to take all these interests into account, and make the difficult choices among conflicting demands, Congress should settle these questions. But if Congress simply sets a goal for an administrative agency, and leaves it to the agency to resolve the competing interests, it is shirking its obligations as a legislature and handing over (or delegating) its exclusive legislative power to an administrative agency that has no legitimate authority to make major decisions of this kind for the nation as a whole.

Supporters of the administrative state cling to the idea that, because the president is elected and administrative agencies are part of the executive branch, this provides some legitimacy to the decisions of administrative agencies. This is a fallacious argument. It is true, of course, that administrative agencies have a connection to the president, an elected official, but that does not cure the basic constitutional infirmity discussed in this book. The issue is not whether administrative agencies have a connection to an elected official, but where such an agency derives its authority to make a particular policy decision. If the policy decision is important enough that it is legislative in nature, the separation of powers *requires* that the decision be made by Congress. (This issue is discussed fully in chapter 6.) On the other hand, if the decision is of lesser importance—akin to filling in the details of a statute enacted by Congress—then it can be made by the administrative agency under the authority of the statute, without any need for presidential approval or endorsement.

Yet, as noted in chapter 3, Congress often fails to perform the role assigned to it by the Constitution—to make the major decisions for society—and leaves important decisions to an administrative agency. Congress is encouraged to follow this easy road for at least two reasons: First, setting a legislative goal can allow members of Congress to take credit for solving a problem, even though they have only transferred the heavy lifting to an administrative agency. When the difficult decisions are made by an agency, members of Congress avoid blame by telling constituents, "I never voted for *that*." Second, it makes little sense for Congress to go through the difficult process of legislating—including all the compromises and hard votes it entails—if courts are not going to hold administrative agencies within the bounds that Congress sets. Chapter 1 describes many cases where administrative agencies have gone well beyond what Congress likely intended, with no intervention by the courts. This is not what the Framers had in mind, and not even what Congress specified in the Administrative Procedure Act (1946), which makes clear that agency decisions are subject to "judicial review."

However, as detailed in this book, the judiciary could force Congress to shoulder its legislative responsibilities simply by determining "what the law is"—that is, looking carefully at whether an administrative agency actually has the statutory authorities it claims. This is what is meant by judicial review, and it can have a salutary effect on Congress itself.

If the courts invalidate an agency's claim of authority, Congress would be required to legislate—that is, to more carefully define the scope of the authority it is conferring and the limits of the agency's discretion.

In this way, by compelling Congress to carry out its responsibilities under the Constitution, the courts would put Congress back in charge of making the laws. To date, when the courts have been presented with this opportunity, they have often demurred. In the absence of judicial intervention, one of the things the Framers feared has actually happened—the growth of a lawgiver in the form of the administrative state that operates outside the direct control of Congress and the judiciary, and is often independent even within the executive branch of which it is nominally a part.

The Failure of the Courts

For well over a hundred years, through a terrible Civil War, the Framers' system worked as planned. But in the 1930s the fortitude of the judiciary seemed to break, and the Supreme Court began to align itself with what Hamilton called "the major voice of the community." Judges and justices came to believe that their role—which the Framers saw as a crucial check on the other branches—was really to give the other branches the widest latitude for action. As the Court stated in *Chevron v. NRDC*:

> When a challenge to an agency construction of a statutory provision, fairly conceptualized, really centers on the wisdom of the agency's policy, rather than whether it is a reasonable choice within a gap left open by Congress, the challenge must fail. In such a case, federal judges—who have no constituency—have a duty to respect legitimate policy choices made by those who do. The responsibilities for assessing the wisdom of such policy choices and resolving the struggle between competing views of the public interest are not judicial ones: "Our Constitution vests such responsibilities in the political branches."[7]

But the issue in *Chevron* was *not* solely a policy choice, which should certainly be left to the political branches; the real question, as discussed in chapter 7, was whether the decision on adopting that policy should have been made by Congress or the administrative agency. That is exactly the kind of issue that the Framers thought the judiciary should address, because it involves the separation of powers. As discussed in chapter 6, the legislative power of Congress is exclusive; it may not be delegated. Thus, if the policy choice was legislative in nature, it was to be made by Congress; if the policy choice was not legislative—subordinate, and thus administrative, in nature—then it could be properly made by an administrative agency. The judiciary was to be the decider on whether Congress had unconstitutionally delegated legislative authority to the agency, or—assuming that an unconstitutional delegation had *not* occurred—whether the agency had gone beyond the authority Congress had granted. In either case, the administrative agency would not have the authority to make the decision.

The *Chevron* Court did not even see the issue; instead, it concluded that, since Congress had not made a decision on the policy question before the agency, Congress *intended* that the agency resolve it—no matter how important to the interests involved. Worse still, the Court took this position because it believed that the decision before it should be made by one of the "political branches." This turns the Framers' constitutional structure on its head. As noted earlier, judges are given lifetime appointments so they can decide, free of political pressures, whether the policy decision should be made by Congress or an administrative agency. *Chevron*, however, says that the decision should be made by the administrative agency simply *because* it is part of an elected branch. The all-important question whether the decision was legislative or administrative seems to have eluded the Court.

Granted, it is difficult to differentiate between a legislative and an administrative matter; but the Framers expected that the judiciary could and would be able to make such distinctions. Anyway, as Justice (then Judge) Neil Gorsuch said in a 2015 case, "the difficulty of the inquiry doesn't mean it isn't worth the effort.... At stake is the principle that the scope of individual liberty may be reduced only according to the deliberately difficult processes prescribed by the Constitution, a principle that may not be fully vindicated without the intervention of the courts."[8] If an administrative agency uses its interpretive power to expand on what

Congress intended, it is, in effect, assuming both the legislative function of Congress and the judicial function of the courts as envisioned by the Framers, thus nullifying the separation of powers. For this reason, the *Chevron* decision, as Gorsuch wrote in 2016, "seems more than a little difficult to square with the Constitution of the Framers' design."[9]

The Administrative State and the Constitution

In general, there is no inconsistency between the constitutional separation of powers and the existence of the administrative state. Although not expressly contemplated by the Framers when they designed the constitutional structure, almost all administrative agencies fit comfortably within the executive branch. The five largest issuers of regulations in 2016 were cabinet departments such as Labor, Treasury, and Health and Human Services; the sixth was the Environmental Protection Agency. In 2017, Commerce, Defense, Transportation, Treasury, and the EPA were among the leaders, accounting for 43 percent of all the rules in the pipeline.[10] The heads of all these agencies are single administrators, appointed by, reporting to, and serving at the pleasure of the president. Under the separation of powers, however, none of these agencies—nor the president himself—has the power to issue regulations other than as authorized by the Constitution specifically or by Congress.

The Securities and Exchange Commission and the Federal Reserve, because they are managed by a bipartisan group appointed for specific terms, might be said to be part of an independent fourth branch not contemplated by the Constitution. But the 2010 Dodd-Frank Act brought these and other federal financial regulators—most of which are managed by multiheaded, bipartisan commissions—under the president's policy direction through membership in the Financial Stability Oversight Council (FSOC), which is chaired by the secretary of the Treasury. Moreover, whatever stigma once attached to the president's direct control of an "independent" agency, it did not survive President Barack Obama's direction to the chairman of the Federal Communications Commission that the agency adopt a policy called "net neutrality" (discussed in chapter 5). In short, during the Obama administration the agencies that used to be called "arms of Congress" or the fourth branch of government have now been folded into the executive branch.

It is not, then, the existence of the administrative state that raises constitutional questions, but rather the uncontrolled nature of the powers that it wields. Increasingly, it seems to be making important decisions that should be made by Congress. Not only does this combine both legislative and executive functions in the same hands—a fundamental concern of the Framers—but it also raises troubling questions about both the continued viability of representative democracy and, as discussed below, the government's very legitimacy.

An American Brexit?

Some undoubtedly will ask, "What's the harm?" If Congress doesn't act, then one of the agencies of the executive branch—or even the president—can step in to make the necessary decisions. What's the problem with that? The question, again, is, in a representative democracy, who decides what should be done—or indeed *whether* it should be done. Most Americans would agree that leaving that decision in the hands of the federal bureaucracy cannot be the answer. Who elected them? What special claim entitles them to make decisions for so many? Even the president, as noted earlier, though elected by the citizenry, cannot be considered fully representative of all the interests that comprise the nation. The only body that could conceivably perform this role is Congress.

Even if bureaucratic decisions do not alarm us today, we have to think about a future in which—if current trends continue—administrative agencies will make most of the major decisions for society. That, unfortunately, is where the nation is heading if there is no effective check on the rulemaking authority of an unrepresentative group of government functionaries that make up the administrative state. Many believe this has already occurred, with administrative agencies dictating who can use what bathroom, disregarding religious convictions, and imposing so many costly regulations that it is difficult to start or finance a new business. We have not perhaps yet reached the point where a majority of the country is dissatisfied with the government—although polling consistently shows the public, by a wide margin, believes the country is on the "wrong track"—but the point will come when a majority no longer believes that the government responds to their wishes, or even listens to them. Indeed, some think that the election of Donald Trump in 2016 sent just such a message.

The sense that government cannot be controlled is new to Americans, and to others used to living in a democracy. In 2016, in a vote nicknamed Brexit, a majority of British voters—despite strong opposition by the British elites—chose to have the United Kingdom leave the European Union. Many factors have been cited as reasons for this extraordinary action, including anti-immigrant feelings, but most likely it would not have occurred had so many Britons not become concerned that their sovereignty—their right to control their own government—was in question.

We can see this clearly in the following excerpts from a speech by Boris Johnson, one of the leaders of the Brexit campaign:

> The biggest myth in this whole [Brexit] debate is that there is some clear division between the arguments about democracy, and the arguments about economics....
>
> For instance there are many reasonable people on the Remain side who are willing to accept that the EU suffers from what has for a long time been acknowledged to be a democratic deficit.
>
> If pushed, they would admit that there are legitimate concerns about the accountability of the [EU] Commission, about the popular legitimacy of the European parliament, and about the increasingly wayward judgments of the European court of justice.
>
> They would accept...that there is something troubling about the sheer volume of EU law, and the way it now contributes 60 per cent of the laws passing through parliament.
>
> They would acknowledge that this vast corpus of EU law is generated by the Brussels commission; and that it is now extremely worrying that only 3.6 per cent of EU Commission officials actually come from this country....

Johnson then enumerated the "disastrous economic consequences" of remaining in the EU:

We are currently unable to exercise democratic control over such basic economic matters as our tax rates....

We cannot exercise democratic control over the energy costs of our steel firms, even when those costs are far higher than in other EU countries—so that companies in this country are going to the wall because of our slavish adherence to EU rules....

We cannot do anything to stop the torrent of EU legislation, coming at a rate of 2,500 a year, and imposing costs of £600m per week on UK business.

We cannot control the EU budget....

We can neither stop other countries going ahead with ill-advised plans to create an economic government of Europe...nor can we protect the UK taxpayer from the demands of the eurozone countries for bail-out funds....

It is time to take back control, and speak for freedom in Britain....[11]

While these complaints do not match up precisely with concerns about the administrative state in the United States, they come close enough to give us a picture of what might happen if Americans at some point come to believe that they are being governed by an unaccountable group that does not share their interests or their outlook.

At the end of 2016, there were 2,419 proposed rules awaiting final action, and by the end of 2017—after a concerted effort by the Trump administration during its first year to reduce regulation—there were still 1,834 rules in the pipeline. While this was a 24 percent decline, it also shows the persistence of the agencies in issuing rules even when the administration in office has made extraordinary efforts to cut down on rulemaking. According to Clyde Wayne Crews of the Competitive Enterprise Institute, who tracks these numbers, the agencies of the administrative state have issued 101,380 rules since 1993, and never less than 3,000 rules in any one year. The number of regulations bears little relationship to the number of laws enacted by Congress. In 2017 Congress enacted 97 laws, but the agencies issued 3,281 rules.[12]

These numbers provide a rough indication of the degree to which the American people are governed by the administrative state rather than the

Congress they elect. True, Congress adopts general laws, and the agencies of the executive branch have to implement them with more specific rules; but as congressional legislation has become more and more general and goal-oriented, and the rules issued by administrative agencies more and more restrictive, the question is who is in fact the lawmaker. In the end, we are dealing with a question of legitimacy: whether the institutions of government are seen by the citizenry as having a moral right to command obedience. Brexit shows that legitimacy is something not to be trifled with.

What This Book Is About

Regulations are constantly being issued, sometimes without the direction of anyone above the senior official of the issuing agency, based on laws passed decades or generations ago. Some may be the legitimate "filling in" of details, but others—several of which are discussed in this book—are explicit or implicit interpretations of the statutory authority and jurisdiction of the agencies that issued them, and these seem to go well beyond the authority that Congress intended to grant.

That is the issue this book addresses. Regulations must be based on some statutory underpinning, but once Congress enacts a statute and the president signs it into law, the latitude provided to administrative agencies by the Supreme Court's decision in *Chevron* provides agencies with almost unfettered authority to determine what the statutory language means. That is where the problems arise, as discussed in chapter 1, on regulation and the rule of law. In most cases, this has occurred because the courts have failed to perform the key responsibility that Chief Justice Marshall articulated in *Marbury*: "It is emphatically the province and duty of the Judicial Department to say what the law is." But there is also a deeper question—whether Congress has allowed the agencies of the administrative state to make the major decisions for society that are supposed to be made by a legislature. That issue—the delegation of its legislative authority by Congress—is discussed in chapter 6. There, I argue that Congress has incentives to avoid making the difficult legislative decisions that, as a legislature, it is required to make under the separation of powers. The unconstitutional delegation of legislative authority can be prevented by the resuscitation of the nondelegation doctrine, which nullifies unconstitutional delegations of legislative authority and will impose the necessary discipline on Congress.

One other point is pertinent here. Questions frequently arise about the constitutionality of a statute. The Supreme Court has said in numerous cases that a regulatory law will not be deemed unconstitutional if it has a "rational basis."[13] The Constitution gives Congress the power to legislate, and it is in the nature of legislation to be arbitrary, highly discretionary, and disappointing to some interests. For this reason, it makes sense for the Court to impose a high hurdle for declaring regulatory laws unconstitutional, and that issue will not be discussed in this book. What will be discussed is not whether the Court has correctly interpreted the *words* of the Constitution, but instead whether it has correctly interpreted its own role and the role of the judiciary in implementing the Constitution's *structure*.

No Reason for Pessimism

Finally, it is reasonable to believe that the Constitution originally designed by the Framers is now gone, and essentially irretrievable. This position is argued persuasively by my American Enterprise Institute colleague Charles Murray in his 2015 book, *By the People*.[14] His thesis is that even the appointment of true Madisonians to the Supreme Court cannot reverse the growth of the government or achieve a restoration of the Constitution as it was ratified in 1788; the American people have simply come to expect much more from their government today than they did as recently as the early twentieth century.

I agree with Murray's view about the growth of the government, and what the American people expect from it today, but I do not agree that the American people are or will be resigned to accepting a government that they cannot influence with their votes. In chapter 5, I discuss several examples where significant deregulation was achieved by Congress in the 1970s and 1980s, bringing major improvements for both the regulated industries and consumers. This shows, in my view, that Murray's pessimism is overstated. The votes of the American people still count, and if they are persuaded that changes in government policies are necessary, those corrections will eventually be made.

Many of the changes in government policies that Murray decries took a long time to put in place, but—with sustained attention to their adverse effects—will also eventually be repealed. The deregulation that has been pressed by a Republican Congress and the Trump administration—while not yet as far-reaching as necessary—shows that change can happen under the Constitution. All that is necessary is that Congress have the incentive to *legislate* in response to public demands. The constitutional system devised by the Framers will fail the American people only if the judiciary continues to allow Congress to pretend to legislate, by passing laws that do not actually make the hard choices that real legislation requires. In that case, the administrative state will increasingly make the key decisions for American society.

Brexit shows that in a democracy the people ultimately govern, and over time they can work their will. The Framers have provided the means for that to happen in the United States. If it is true that the people want more from government than the Framers expected, the Constitution gives Congress the power to provide it by making decisions that the administrative agencies can enforce through rules and regulations. But it is important for the courts to ensure that administrative rules do not transcend the intent or scope of what Congress actually enacted. If this happens, as in Brexit, we too will eventually have a crisis of legitimacy.

In this connection, while it is somewhat early to tell, it looks as though the first serious questioning of *Chevron* is occurring on the Supreme Court. As discussed in chapter 7, in recent cases, at least three justices—John Roberts, Samuel Alito, and Clarence Thomas—have expressed reservations about the scope of *Chevron* deference. Justice Gorsuch, appointed to the Court in 2017, also questioned *Chevron* when he was an appellate judge, writing, as noted above, that the *Chevron* decision "seems more than a little difficult to square with the Constitution of the Framers' design." As this is written, President Trump has nominated Judge Brett Kavanaugh to take Justice Anthony Kennedy's seat on the Supreme Court. From all indications, Judge Kavanaugh's positions on *Chevron* and the role of the courts in the separation of powers are close to those of Justice Gorsuch. Thus, if he is confirmed by the Senate, there is likely to be a Supreme Court majority in favor of modifying *Chevron*. This in itself will slow the growth of the administrative state.

Perhaps even more important, however, while supporting a narrower interpretation of *Chevron* in a 2013 case, Chief Justice John Roberts, in a dissent joined by Justices Kennedy and Alito, noted: "But there is another concern at play, no less firmly rooted in our constitutional structure. *This is the obligation of the Judiciary not only to confine itself to its proper role, but to ensure that the other branches do as well.*"[15] This can only be a reference to the nondelegation doctrine, discussed in chapter 6, the resuscitation of which will require Congress—and only Congress—to make the major policy choices for society.

Since 2013 the changes in the Court have substantially increased the likelihood that some version of the nondelegation doctrine will be resuscitated. Chief Justice Roberts and Justice Alito hinted as much in this dissent, and Justice Thomas has made his views clear on this point in other concurrences. Justice Gorsuch and Judge Kavanaugh have not spoken directly on the question, but both are known for their support for the separation of powers. As noted in chapter 6, it is difficult if not impossible to defend the separation of powers without a viable nondelegation doctrine.

1

THE ADMINISTRATIVE STATE AND THE RULE OF LAW

It will be of little avail to the people, that the laws are made by men of their own choice, if the laws be so voluminous that they cannot be read, or so incoherent that they cannot be understood; if they be repealed or revised before they are promulgated, or undergo such incessant changes that no man, who knows what the law is to-day, can guess what it will be to-morrow. Law is defined to be a rule of action; but how can that be a rule, which is little known, and less fixed?

JAMES MADISON, *FEDERALIST* NO. 62

We live, we believe, in a country governed by the rule of law, and recognize that this is in large part responsible for the success of our country and the well-being of its citizens. In our diverse and complex society, with many competing interests, a framework of laws to guide individual actions is essential; people know what to expect and what is expected of them. This framework breaks down, however, when agencies of the administrative state formulate regulations that go beyond the authority they have been given by Congress.

In *The Road to Serfdom*, Friedrich Hayek points out that it is wrong to believe that the rule of law exists in a society simply because all the actions of the state are duly authorized by legislation. He writes that the rule of law "has little to do with the question whether all actions of government are legal in the juridical sense. They may well be and yet not conform to the Rule of Law.... If the law says that ... a board or authority may do what it pleases, anything that board or authority does

I

is legal—but its actions are certainly not subject to the Rule of Law."[1] To Hayek, "the important question is whether the individual can foresee the action of the state and make use of this knowledge as a datum in forming his own plans...or whether the state is in a position to frustrate individual efforts."[2]

Justice Clarence Thomas made the same point in his important concurring opinion in *Perez v. Mortgage Bankers Association*, a case that dealt with the validity of a Labor Department change in its interpretation of the wage and hour laws. Thomas noted that one of the justifications for providing judicial deference to agency interpretations of their rules is that "agencies are better suited to define the original intent behind their regulations." However, he wrote, "[i]t is the text of the regulations that have the force and effect of law, not the agency's intent. Citizens arrange their affairs not on the basis of their legislators' unexpressed intent, but on the basis of the law as it is written and promulgated....To be governed by legislated text rather than legislators' intentions is what it means to be a Government of laws, not of men."[3]

This is the standard we should be looking for when we analyze what administrative agencies do: not whether there is some justification in the authorizing statute for a particular regulation, but whether Congress intended, at the time it enacted the statute, to give the agency the powers it is asserting. In other words, has the agency moved beyond the task of administering or enforcing the law into the role of making law, reserved by the Constitution to Congress?

The Consumer Financial Protection Bureau

It is useful to begin this discussion of regulation and the rule of law with the Consumer Financial Protection Bureau (CFPB), a glaring example of an agency that seemed, during the Obama administration, to have little regard for the rule of law. Most of the problems associated with the agencies of the administrative state arise from agencies issuing regulations that exceed the authority they were given by Congress. This is an obvious violation of the rule of law. However, the CFPB was different: it refused to prescribe rules or regulations that would restrict or limit its freedom to bring enforcement actions. In other words, it set out not to gain compliance by the regulated industry with any set of rules but instead to punish what it saw as inherent wrongdoing, apart from any set of rules.

Administrative and regulatory agencies have authority to make rules for two reasons: first, to fill in the details of what Congress authorized, and second, to inform those subject to their jurisdiction about how to conform their activities to the new policies embodied in the statute. The CFPB, established under the Dodd-Frank Act, is an example of an agency (at least in the Obama administration) that had less interest in providing information about the rules it would enforce than in gaining publicity through enforcement actions. In that sense, the agency is a prime example of how a regulatory agency can use its statutory authority to go beyond what Congress intended and, in doing so, impair the rule of law in a different way.

To be sure, some of the sponsors of the CFPB's statutory foundation said the agency should be an enforcement agency and not a regulatory agency. By this, they might have meant that the CFPB should do most of its work through enforcement actions rather than through regulations. This would not be wrong if the agency had first established the rules that it would enforce, but that is not how it proceeded. Among other things, the agency was empowered to prevent "abuse" of consumers, but its director during the Obama administration, Richard Cordray, refused to provide any guidance on what constitutes "abuse,"[4] asserting instead that he intended to define the term through enforcement actions.[5] Contrast this approach with that of the Securities and Exchange Commission. The SEC spends most of its resources on enforcement, but had first laid down a comprehensive set of rules to guide the behavior of those in the securities industry who wanted to operate within the rules.

Enforcement actions without an underlying set of rules is a derogation of the rule of law, since a regulated firm can have no idea what activities might constitute abuse and thus no way to modify its behavior. As Mick Mulvaney, the acting director who succeeded Cordray, noted in a memorandum to the CFPB staff: "the people we regulate should have the right to know what the rules are before being charged with breaking them."[6] Moreover, the effect of Cordray's approach to enforcement is more likely to harm consumers and the regulated industry than to help them. As Todd Zywicki, a law professor, notes, "The ability to deem certain products as inherently unsafe or 'abusive' is a dangerous one that will likely chill innovation and the introduction of new products."[7]

The CFPB also provides an example of how an agency, in the absence of any judicial review, can arrogate to itself authorities that were denied in its authorizing statute. This is often possible because the regulated industry is afraid to challenge an aggressive agency, and could well suffer reputational harm when accused of bilking consumers. Although the Dodd-Frank Act provided the CFPB with a broad mandate to protect consumers against "unfair, deceptive or abusive acts and practices," it clearly exempted auto financing from the scope of the agency's authority. "Nonetheless," as recounted by Neomi Rao, a scholar of administrative law who heads the Office of Management and Budget's Office of Information and Regulatory Affairs (OIRA) in the Trump administration, "the CFPB...enacted a rule to cover nonbank auto finance companies.... The Bureau relied on its general authority to supervise nonbank 'larger participant[s] of a market for other consumer financial products or services' as the Bureau defines by rule."[8] In other words, the agency used its general and open-ended authority to trump specific statutory limitations and leverage itself into the regulation of auto lenders.

Needless to say, if the touchstone of the rule of law is the language that Congress actually enacts, and if that language is ignored by administrative agencies, even statutes become unreliable guideposts for those who try to conform their behavior to what the law requires. Mulvaney's memorandum to CFPB staff should be a mission statement for every regulatory agency: "I intend to exercise our statutory authority to enforce the laws of this nation. But we will no longer go beyond that mandate. If Congress wants us to do more than is set forth in the Dodd-Frank Act, they can change the law. Until then, we will enforce the law as currently written."[9]

Title IX and Sexual Harassment

Another example of administrative actions that go well beyond Congress's intent is the Education Department's interpretation of the following language in Title IX of the Education Amendments of 1972: "No person in the United States shall, on the basis of sex, be excluded from participation in, be denied the benefits of, or be subjected to discrimination under any education program or activity receiving Federal financial assistance."

This language, which Congress almost certainly meant to apply to discrimination against women in the provision of educational resources, was first interpreted by a federal court to cover the failure of a school to respond to allegations of sexual harassment by professors.[10] The court reasoned that denial of educational resources because of refusal to accede to sexual demands came within the statutory language. But what was spun out from this rationale went even further beyond what Congress could have had in mind. In 1975 the predecessor of the Education Department issued a rule that applied Title IX to employment discrimination. This was upheld by the Supreme Court in 1982. In 1977 the department applied its regulations under Title IX to a school that received federal financial assistance only indirectly, through education grants to students. This was upheld by the Supreme Court in 1984.

Interpretations like this could conceivably have been within the contemplation of Congress, but it was the success of the Education Department's Office of Civil Rights (OCR) in turning what had been devised by Congress as an antidiscrimination law into an anti-sexual-harassment law that is the most remarkable example of how administrative agencies can manipulate their statutory mandates.

In granting rulemaking authority to the Department of Education, Congress took an unusual step: it required that any rules under Title IX had to be signed by the president. Indeed, the first rule, after much negotiation, was signed by President Gerald Ford in 1975, but that was the last time that the department followed the normal requirement under the Administrative Procedure Act to issue a proposed rule, solicit public comments, and issue a final rule with responses to the comments received. As R. Shep Melnick reports in his comprehensive book on Title IX, "OCR has evaded [the statutory] requirements by labeling its commands 'interpretations,' 'clarifications,' and 'guidance' rather than 'rules,' and denying—quite unconvincingly—that they did anything new. In recent years it has announced major policy decisions in Dear

Colleague Letters,…inverting standard rulemaking procedures by asking for comments only after it has established its position."[11]

These documents are not strictly binding on the educational institutions on which they have been imposed, but as Melnick notes, OCR "warned schools that they will face serious sanctions if they fail to comply with the mandates contained in these documents."[12] This cavalier treatment of the rulemaking process cannot be consistent with the rule of law. And it gets worse when we look at what OCR has been requiring since 1975 with its unauthorized commands. In effect, largely without objection by the courts, it has usurped the power of Congress by creating rules on sexual harassment for educational institutions that have no basis in law but have resulted in serious punishments for students caught in this *ultra vires* web.

The link between the discrimination by an educational institution that was prohibited by the underlying statute, and the peer-to-peer sexual harassment OCR set out to prevent, was the concept of the "hostile environment." This allowed OCR to threaten schools with penalties even when the harassment occurred between students. According to Melnick,

> the first reported decision on school liability for student-on-student harassment appeared in 1993. By 1998 there were twenty-four published federal district court decisions on the subject, as well as rulings by six circuit courts…. Federal courts were all over the map on the liability standard to apply. Some ruled that schools were liable if they "knew or should have known" about behavior that created the hostile environment. Others held that schools would be held responsible only if they had "actual knowledge" of the behavior and failed to take corrective action.[13]

There is no indication that any court questioned how a statute that prohibited discrimination by schools "on the basis of sex" had become a vehicle for punishing student-on-student sexual harassment—and how all of this had been done without a notice-and-comment rulemaking.

Matters got even worse as OCR—essentially uninhibited by courts—went about defining "sexual harassment." The scope of the law's application continued to grow. In 1994 OCR sent a letter to Santa Rosa

Junior College agreeing with two students at the California school who had claimed that sexually oriented offensive speech had created a "hostile educational environment" and directing the college to adopt a policy to prevent it. Although the Supreme Court held in one case that student-on-student sexual harassment had to be "so severe, pervasive and objectively offensive that it can be said to deprive victims of access to educational opportunities,"[14] by 2008 the Office of Civil Rights was defining sexual harassment as "unwelcome" sexual conduct and "telling sexual or dirty jokes."[15] It is highly unlikely that Congress would have adopted this rule in 1972, especially in light of its implications for First Amendment rights.

With the advent of the Obama administration, the Office of Civil Rights became even more aggressive in its use of this law. In April 2011 it issued another letter, to the effect that schools must respond to claims of sexual harassment with a grievance procedure that uses a "preponderance of the evidence" standard. For a penalty that could lead to expulsion from an academic institution, a life-changing event, a preponderance of the evidence standard means that the accused can be convicted even though there is reasonable doubt concerning guilt. Nor is there any indication in Title IX that the department can require such an evidentiary standard.

In its 2013 agreement with the University of Montana, which the department referred to as "a blueprint for colleges and universities," the department and the university agreed that sexual harassment should be defined as "any unwelcome conduct of a sexual nature,"[16] and in an accompanying May 9, 2015, letter to the university, the Departments of Justice and Education noted that sexual harassment need not be "objectively offensive."[17] Under this standard, the important question is whether the complainant was offended—and thus sexually harassed—not whether a reasonable person would be offended.

This is an egregious example of how legislative language can be perverted into something unrecognizable because of compliant courts and no standards about how to interpret existing legislation. Starting with a simple and sensible idea—that no one should be deprived of the benefits of a federally supported educational institution because of sex or other discrimination—we now have a system in which normal communications between college students, protected by the First Amendment, are potentially punishable with expulsion. Clearly, something has gone seriously wrong. Congress enacts legislation, and the agencies and courts change Congress's initial grant of legislative authority to conform to what *they* want. This is not the rule of law, and the courts are complicit in it.

But the story does not end there. OCR had become so accustomed to having its ukases accepted by educational institutions and courts that it decided, in effect, to redefine the meaning of the word "sex" in Title IX. The statute prohibited discrimination in the provision of educational facilities "on the basis of sex." In this context, "sex" obviously meant biological sex—the difference between male and female; it was clearly intended to equalize the treatment of the two sexes. But in January 2015, OCR in effect declared that it really meant that schools had to accommodate the "sexual orientation" or "gender identity" of each individual.

In a letter responding to a transgender advocate—again, not a formal regulation based on the notice and comment procedure required by the APA—OCR stated, "When a school elects to separate or treat students differently on the basis of sex" it "must treat transgender students consistent with their gender identity," which of course can be different from their biological sex. This idea became known as the "bathroom" case, but in principle it went further than that. OCR's interpretations of its authority—especially during the Obama administration—were exceedingly aggressive. This particular interpretation could mean that an anatomical male who identifies as female could use the showers in the locker room reserved for women in a school's athletic facilities. Not to permit this, according to OCR, would be discrimination on the basis of sex, and violate Title IX.

In the first case based on this interpretation of Title IX's application to a transgender boy (an anatomical female who identified as a male), the district court dismissed the suit, but the Fourth Circuit reversed the dismissal on the basis that OCR's interpretation of its own presidentially approved 1975 regulation is entitled to deference. This is known as *Auer* deference, and discussed elsewhere, but the court did not seem to recognize that what it called a regulation was a very general statement that did not go substantially beyond the language of the statute, and had been supplemented over more than forty years by administrative interpretations that had—without significant objection by the courts—enlarged the scope and coverage of the statutory language.

Thus we see that the courts will defer to an administrative decision that is based on nothing more than an informal interpretation of a series of policy decisions, which themselves were highly questionable expansions of the language in the underlying statute. Shortly after taking office, the Trump administration withdrew the OCR bathroom ruling, but given the willingness of the court system over many years to defer to the increasingly aggressive interpretations of Title IX by OCR, it is hard to believe that another administration will not resurrect this idea in the future. In these circumstances, where does the rule of law reside?

The Regulators, the Justice Department, and Operation Choke Point

Agency action can be even more egregious, especially when it occurs under a policy established with the approval of the Justice Department. The power to regulate—in addition to the power to tax—is the power to destroy. In a number of ways, the Obama administration was more interested in achieving certain policy goals than in punctilious compliance with the law.[18] One especially noteworthy example of this misuse of regulatory power, going well beyond any clear legal authority granted by Congress, was the Justice Department's "Operation Choke Point," a plan designed to choke off the operation of disfavored businesses by using bank regulation to deprive them of operating funds and other financial services. This goes beyond perverting the law into using regulatory power for overtly political purposes.

The facts associated with this action demonstrate that administrative violations of the rule of law can consist of more than simply stretching statutory language to cover subjects—like "abuse" of consumers—that are not defined in advance. In Operation Choke Point, with the approval or at the behest of the Obama administration's Department of Justice, the bank regulatory agencies directed banks to cease making loans, or in some cases cease to provide any banking services, to payday lenders and others in disfavored but wholly legal industries.

The statutes under which bank regulators are authorized to maintain the safety and soundness of insured banks prescribe general standards for the operation and management of a bank, for maintaining asset quality, and for compensation of officers, directors, and employees.[19] In addition to specific requirements, the agencies are given broad authority to set whatever standards they "determine to be appropriate," but none of these standards suggests that the agencies may prohibit a bank from making a loan to a particular category of borrower.

A staff report of the House of Representatives Committee on Oversight and Government Reform reported in 2014 that the Federal Deposit Insurance Corporation (FDIC), one of the agencies involved in Operation Choke Point, had designated thirty types of "high-risk merchants," including sellers of firearms and ammunition, coin dealers, sellers of lottery tickets, money transfer networks, and payday lenders, for curtailed banking services, including cutting off funding.[20]

Given the importance of banks to the development of the economy and the financing of business, the power to prescribe the categories of borrowers that would be eligible for receiving a bank loan would be to place a life-or-death power over legitimate businesses in the hands of bank regulators. It is impossible to imagine that any Congress would give a power like this to any regulator or group of regulators.

Payday lenders were a particular target. Although Operation Choke Point began in 2012, it took some time for victims to realize what was happening to them; they were not generally told by the banks—fearful of retaliation by their regulators—why their banking services were being terminated. Eventually, it became clear that this was an Obama administration program, organized and coordinated by the administration's Justice Department. In 2015 several payday lenders brought an action (*Advance America v. FDIC*) in the D.C. Federal District Court against the FDIC, the Comptroller of the Currency (the regulator of national banks), the Federal Reserve Board, and the Department of Justice as the instigator of the program.

In denying the government's motion for summary judgment, the trial court found that the allegations of the plaintiff payday lenders were accurate—the bank regulators, supported by the Justice Department, had in fact forced banks into denying services to the plaintiffs:

> It is undisputed that the [Plaintiffs] have already lost bank accounts . . . and Plaintiffs have alleged sufficient facts to plausibly tie these losses to the actions of the Federal Defendants under the auspices of Operation Chokepoint. If those losses continue, it is certainly plausible that the [Plaintiffs] will effectively be cut off from the banking system and/or put out of business.[21]

This episode demonstrates that one of the dangers of allowing agencies to decide the extent of their statutory authorities is the arrogance that comes from not having to answer to anyone, least of all the courts. The fact that the administration's illegal plan was ultimately overturned by a court is the exception that proves the value of the rule. The outcome might have been different if the judge in this case, Gladys Kessler of the D.C. Federal District Court, did not have life tenure under the Constitution's Article III. This is also an example of the potential danger to liberty, recognized by the Framers, when a legislative body (a bank regulator with legislative-like power) is not independent of the executive authority.

The Environmental Protection Agency and Greenhouse Gases

The Environmental Protection Agency (EPA) has been a particularly aggressive interpreter of its statutory authority under the Clean Air Act. Under the act's Title V, the EPA is authorized to regulate the emission of various pollutants, such as sulfur dioxide and carbon monoxide, by large stationary sources. These emitters must have permits and are subject to special additional regulation, including expensive mitigation equipment.

In a 2007 case, *Massachusetts v. Environmental Protection Agency*, the Supreme Court decided that Title II of the Clean Air Act authorized the EPA to regulate "greenhouse gases," primarily carbon dioxide (CO_2), emitted by new motor vehicles.[22] The EPA interpreted this decision very broadly, believing that it could now treat CO_2 as an air pollutant along with the others that had previously been designated; it issued a final regulation in 2010 that treated CO_2 as a pollutant like those that it was explicitly authorized to regulate for large stationary sources under Title V.

This approach created an administrative problem for the EPA. If CO_2 were treated as a pollutant, it would substantially multiply the number of firms that would be considered large stationary sources; thousands of firms so defined would then be required to get permits and install expensive mitigation equipment. To prevent this result, the EPA arbitrarily set 100,000 tons of CO_2 as the level that would qualify a stationary source as a large emitter, far above the statutory 250 tons set by Congress for other pollutants. In other words, rather than go back to Congress with the new classification of CO_2 as a pollutant, the agency sought to change the tonnage that would classify a firm as a large emitter in the case of CO_2.

The EPA's decision was challenged in *Utility Air Regulatory Group v. Environmental Protection Agency*, and eventually reached the Supreme Court. The Court, in a decision written by Justice Antonin Scalia, disagreed with the EPA, holding that "EPA's interpretation is not permissible":

> EPA's interpretation is...unreasonable because it would bring about an enormous and transformative expansion in EPA's regulatory authority without clear congressional authorization....An agency has no power to "tailor" legislation to bureaucratic policy goals by rewriting unambiguous statutory terms. Agencies exercise discretion only in the interstices created by statutory silence or ambiguity; they must always "'give effect to the unambiguously expressed intent of Congress'"....It is hard to imagine a statutory term less ambiguous than the precise numerical thresholds [in the Clean Air Act]. When EPA replaced those numbers with others of its own choosing, it went well beyond the "bounds of its statutory authority."[23]

What is remarkable about the EPA's action here is that the EPA actually thought it could adopt an interpretation of the Clean Air Act that would extend its authority—but then exempt a large group of emitters whose inclusion would be politically troublesome, all without going back to Congress. Although the Court did not say this, the point the Court was trying to make is that in the context of the Clean Air Act the size of the emission is a critical factor; it is a major issue of policy, the kind of decision that has to be made by Congress. The EPA could not simply adjust its regulations to make it easier to apply its new rule without going back to Congress. The EPA's effort to treat greenhouse gas emissions as pollutants went so far beyond the authorizing statute that it received a rare dressing down by the Supreme Court:

> Under our system of government, Congress makes laws and the President, acting at times through agencies like EPA, "faithfully execute[s]" them.... The power of executing the laws necessarily includes both authority and responsibility to resolve some questions left open by Congress that arise during the law's administration. But it does not include a power to revise clear statutory terms that turn out not to work in practice.... ([An] agency [lacks] authority "to develop new guidelines or to assign liability in a manner inconsistent with" an "unambiguous statute").[24]

Still, even with this rebuke by the Court's majority, the decision was 5–4, showing that four justices were willing at least to give the EPA the leeway both to regulate carbon dioxide as a pollutant and to establish an amount of emissions that would subject a firm to regulation as a large emitter. As Justice Stephen Breyer noted in his dissent: "Judge Learned Hand pointed out when interpreting another statute many years ago, '[w]e can best reach the meaning here, as always, by recourse to the underlying purpose, and, with that as a guide, by trying to project upon the specific occasion how we think persons, actuated by such a purpose, would have dealt with it, if it had been presented to them at the time.'"[25] In other words, in the view of the dissenters in *Utility Air*, the *purpose* of the statute when enacted was sufficient to justify what the EPA had done. Their theory was that if Congress, when the Clean Air Act was adopted, had been presented with whether to regulate a greenhouse gas such as carbon dioxide, it is likely to have done so, and in the way the EPA did it.

This is a fundamental difference in outlook between the majority and the dissenters. The majority read the law strictly by its words; the dissenters would have read it in terms of its purposes. The question raised in this book is which reading most closely adheres to the rule of law. Would an entrepreneur be at substantial risk of a loss of his investment if the administrative agency charged with implementing the statute were allowed to read the statute according to the intent, rather than the words, of Congress? If administrative agencies were allowed to read their statutory authorities according to what the text implied about some possible purpose of Congress—rather than what the words of the text meant at the time they were enacted—statutory language could never be a satisfactory guide to behavior that is necessary for the rule of law.

The Supreme Court and "Disparate Impact"

The Civil Rights Act of 1964 outlawed discrimination on the basis of sex, religion, race, and other factors.[26] A 1971 Supreme Court case, *Griggs v. Duke Power*, tested the validity of a ruling by the Equal Employment Opportunity Commission (EEOC) that racial discrimination could be shown without an actual finding of intent to discriminate.[27] The agency argued that the requirement for equal employment opportunity was violated when a facially neutral employment requirement, such as a high school diploma, had a "disparate impact" on particular groups. The employment requirement must have a relationship to the job involved, the agency argued, and a requirement for a high school diploma, where it was not necessary for the job involved, could have a discriminatory effect on African-Americans whose educational attainments were lower than that of their white counterparts.

The Supreme Court upheld this theory, going beyond the specific language of the statute. "The administrative interpretation of the law by the enforcing agency," said the Court, "is entitled to great deference."[28] This was a considerable step beyond then-current law, and would have major societal and economic effects as plaintiffs sought to show that one test or another—although facially nondiscriminatory—actually disfavors a complaining group. Considering its importance, this is a decision that should have been made by Congress, not an administrative agency.

The consequences of the *Griggs* decision are becoming apparent. In a 5–4 decision in 2015, in *Texas Dept. of Housing and Community Affairs v. Inclusive Communities Project, Inc.*, the Supreme Court found that a variety of other laws, including the Civil Rights Act of 1964, the Age Discrimination and Employment Act of 1967, and the "results-oriented language" of the Fair Housing Act, justified the Court's conclusion to uphold a determination by the Department of Housing and Urban Development (HUD) that disparate impact was a sufficient basis for finding a violation of the fair housing laws. "Together," said the majority, "*Griggs* holds…that antidiscrimination laws must be construed to encompass disparate-impact claims when their text refers to the consequences of actions and not just to the mindset of actors, and where that interpretation is consistent with statutory purpose."[29]

The consequences of this decision for the rule of law are incalculable. How can any business that offers a product or service in a facially neutral way ever know whether its offer will, in effect, discriminate against some protected group or class? Let's assume that an automobile dealer advertises cars, but only in English. Could this be discriminatory with respect to Spanish speakers—either because they don't understand English or because they regard the ads as intended to exclude them as purchasers? What if a bank were to offer mortgages only for homes that cost more than $500,000—would that be discriminatory toward low-income or minority would-be home buyers? From the standpoint of a business, there is almost nothing one can do that can't be regarded as having a disparate impact on one group or another.

Justice Thomas, among the four dissenters (the others were Roberts, Scalia, and Alito) summarized the issue well:

> I write separately to point out that the foundation on which the Court builds its latest disparate-impact regime [citing *Griggs*] is made of sand. That decision, which concluded that Title VII of the Civil Rights Act of 1964 authorizes plaintiffs to bring disparate-impact claims,…represents the triumph of an agency's preferences over Congress' enactment and of assumption over fact. Whatever respect *Griggs* merits as a matter of *stare decisis*, I would not amplify its error by importing its disparate-impact scheme into yet another statute.[30]

He continued: "We should drop the pretense that *Griggs'* interpretation of Title VII was legitimate. 'The Civil Rights Act of 1964 did not include an express prohibition on policies or practices that produce a disparate impact.'"[31]

Regrettably, the foregoing are not isolated examples. In the absence of strict judicial review of laws with broad authorizing language, administrative agencies have continued to use statutory authorities in ways Congress likely never intended. In a 2015 case, for example, the EEOC argued that a company's recruitment on campuses was a form of age discrimination. In 2016 the Education Department's Office of Civil Rights set off a huge controversy with a "Dear Colleague" letter advising schools that receive federal funds that they could lose those funds if they did not allow transgender students to use the bathroom of their choice. OCR clearly thought it had statutory authority to do this, even though later efforts in states to address the issue found that it was too fraught with controversy to resolve legislatively.

Yet another "Dear Colleague" letter, issued jointly in 2014 by the Justice Department and OCR and based on the same general theory as the bathroom letter, notified schools that they were in danger of violating federal law if their disciplinary actions against students showed racial bias.

In 2015 the EPA and the Army Corps of Engineers issued a new rule that substantially broadened its definition of "navigable waters." The new rule covered ditches, ponds, streams, and wetlands that the issuing agencies believed would have an adverse effect on the "navigable waters" that were initially the only waters covered in the Clean Water Act.[32] This enabled the agency to impose fines on people who had ponds and dry streambeds on their property, never imagining that these small water bodies could be included in the phrase "navigable waters." Enforcement of the new rule was enjoined by the Court of Appeals for the Sixth Circuit, and in 2017 the Trump administration ordered steps to begin to repeal the rule.

All these examples show that agencies of the administrative state believe they have considerable power to go beyond the language of the laws they enforce. This is because the courts, over the years—through *Chevron* deference and otherwise—have given these agencies the impression that excursions beyond the four corners of their authorizing statutes will not be questioned. This impression also has the effect of reducing challenges to agency decisions, as counsel advise their clients that efforts to overturn seemingly baseless rules will be unsuccessful. Under these circumstances, it is difficult to say that in the United States today the rule of law inevitably prevails.

The Food and Drug Administration and Tobacco

Most of the cases discussed above involve administrative agencies going beyond any reasonable interpretation of their authorizing statutes, often with no objection by the courts. One of the more unusual examples of administrative overreach was the Food and Drug Administration's claim in 1996 that tobacco was a drug and thus could be regulated by the FDA. This was a reversal of the agency's previous position and was inconsistent with legislation Congress had adopted over many years following the enactment of the Food, Drug, and Cosmetic Act (1938). Moreover, in a 2000 case it seemed unlikely to a majority of the Supreme Court that Congress could have intended to allow an administrative agency to terminate a major industry in the United States without any action by Congress itself:

> Taken together...actions by Congress over the past 35 years preclude an interpretation of the [Food, Drug, and Cosmetic Act] that grants the FDA jurisdiction to regulate tobacco products...Congress has been aware of tobacco's health hazards and its pharmacological effects.... Further, Congress has persistently acted to preclude a meaningful role for *any* administrative agency in making policy on the subject of tobacco and health.... This is hardly an ordinary case. Contrary to its representations to Congress since 1914, the FDA has now asserted jurisdiction to regulate an industry constituting a significant portion of the American economy. In fact, the FDA contends that, were it to determine that tobacco products provide no "reasonable assurance of safety," it would have the authority to ban cigarettes and smokeless tobacco entirely.[33]

Accordingly, the Court affirmed the decision of the Fourth Circuit that the FDA did not have the requisite authority to issue the regulation under consideration.

The importance of this case for the argument presented here is that it demonstrates that the courts can and do step in when administrative agencies go beyond their remit. Still, this was a relatively easy case. The language of the statute was certainly broad enough to encompass the decision of the FDA, but the Court was right to conclude that Congress would never have countenanced the elimination of the tobacco business at the time the statute was drafted. It was a major reach for the FDA to claim that, despite silence in the statute on the issue, it was given authority by Congress to close down an important part of the U.S. economy. The fact that the agency previously had taken the view that it did not have authority to regulate tobacco surely helped the majority's analysis, and it also enabled the majority to develop the idea that Congress had adopted an alternative method of addressing tobacco risk through disclosure to consumers.

Still, where was the rule of law in the FDA's decision? It was obvious that, no matter the health issues associated with tobacco use, there was an enormous business in tobacco products in the United States. An effort by the FDA to outlaw tobacco was bound to upset millions of suppliers and farmers who had made investments in the business on the assumption that it was fully lawful. Yet the FDA thought it could use its statutory authority—which it had previously held did not cover tobacco—to regulate the business. If the agency thought the issue was so important that a reversal of its previous rule was necessary, why didn't it recognize that Congress was the appropriate venue in which to raise the issue? Of course, the effort would be fruitless, at least at first, but it is telling that an administrative agency could have thought that it had the authority to take a step of this significance—upsetting vast areas of the U.S. economy—without congressional authority.

By concluding that Congress did not intend to give the FDA authority to regulate the use of tobacco, the Supreme Court performed the role that the Framers assigned to the judiciary in the constitutional structure. This task should not be minimized; it is very difficult to determine whether a grant of authority should be deemed to cover a set of facts that Congress never contemplated. But it is essential for the rule of law that the courts, rather than administrative agencies themselves, make this commonsense decision. By turning down the agency's decision, the

Court in effect returned the important question to the place where it belonged—in Congress.

Should the Judiciary Discipline the Agencies of the Administrative State?

The Court's decision in the tobacco case could be seen as inconsistent with *Chevron,* the 1984 case that required the courts to defer to an agency's interpretation of its statutory authorities, if the interpretation was deemed to be "reasonable." *Chevron* in effect gave administrative agencies the authority to determine the scope of their authority. As discussed extensively in chapter 7, there have been indications in recent Supreme Court decisions that what is called *Chevron* deference will be circumscribed or eliminated. The cases discussed in this chapter make it obvious that, without strict judicial oversight, the agencies of the administrative state pose a continual challenge to the rule of law.

Other than the tobacco case, and the district court's decision in *Advance America,* the 2017 case concerning Operation Choke Point, the pattern throughout this discussion has been the frequent failure of the courts to discipline the agencies of the administrative state. The plain language of Title IX of the Education Act amendments has been distorted so that the Department of Education now endorses penalizing free speech; the Fair Housing Act now includes unwritten language about disparate impact; the CFPB believes it can expand its authority on auto lending beyond what Congress clearly sought to limit; and the EPA felt free to change one of the key terms of the Clean Air Act—all without consulting Congress. The above examples all raise a question whether the rule of law—in the sense that citizens can know what the laws are and can adjust their behavior accordingly—fully exists in the United States today.

Most defenders of the administrative state would contend that it has grown in importance and effect because the U.S. economy and society have become more complex. Congress, they argue, cannot deal with this complexity, and so was compelled to hand more and more authority to the agencies of the administrative state. There is certainly some truth in this, but as this book argues, the problem of excessive regulation and growth of the administrative state is not a result of the complexity of the economy and society but of the failure of the judiciary to hold administrative agencies to the precise terms of their statutory authorities. Without that restraint, the agencies have strong incentives to reach beyond the bounds of what Congress authorized.

As discussed in chapter 5, the agencies of the administrative state may well have incentives to increase their power and their funding by issuing new regulations. Their ability to do this is enabled by both Congress and the courts—first because Congress has failed in many instances to create legislation that clearly circumscribes what administrative agencies can do, and second because the courts have failed to play their assigned constitutional role as a check on the other two branches of government. Indeed, as covered in chapter 3, the timidity of the courts has given Congress incentives to take the easy way out—adopting open-ended, standardless legislation like the Clean Air Act—when addressing difficult societal problems. If the courts were not so willing to let administrative agencies control the interpretation of these statutes, Congress might be more willing to do the difficult work of crafting legislative compromises. Members of the House and Senate might well wonder why they go through the difficult and time-consuming legislative process if the courts routinely bless whatever interpretation the administrative agency places on the language Congress ultimately chooses.

The United States is a highly complex society, and Congress clearly struggles to meet the demands for updated or new legislation. However, the fact that Congress cannot comply with these demands is not a reason to rely on nondemocratic means to effect change. The reason that Congress has difficulty acting is that the country is often divided about the need for new laws or major changes in policies, and that means they should not be enacted until a majority—speaking through Congress—can agree on the change. Congressional legislation is still the best and only way in our democracy to assure that the voices of all Americans are heard when laws are being made.

Allowing administrative agencies to make rules that they believe are what the public wants or needs is also obviously unsatisfactory. If the rule of law exists, governmental action must be undertaken pursuant to statute. The complexity of a modern society is not a sufficient reason to abandon the constitutional structure in order to give administrative agencies free rein. Hayek had it right when he wrote the following, in *The Constitution of Liberty*:

> What is required under the rule of law is that a court should have the power to decide whether the law provided for a particular action that an authority has taken. In other words, in all instances where administrative action interferes with the private sphere of the individual, the courts must have the power to decide not only whether a particular action was *infra vires* or *ultra vires* but whether the substance of the administrative decision was such as the law demanded. It is only if this is the case that administrative discretion is precluded.[34]

2

THE SEPARATION OF POWERS AND CHECKS AND BALANCES

When courts refuse even to decide what the best interpretation is under the law, they abandon the judicial check. That abandonment permits precisely the accumulation of governmental powers that the Framers warned against.

JUSTICE CLARENCE THOMAS[1]

Only the United States, among large and developed countries, has a written constitution that divides its government into three distinct parts—a Congress with responsibilities for legislation, a president to execute the laws, and a judiciary to interpret the laws. The Framers seem to have had two reasons for this complex structure. First, as always, was the paramount goal of preserving liberty for the American people: the Framers' central stated purpose was to make it as difficult as possible for the government to threaten these freedoms. In *Federalist* No. 47, Madison states the Framers' theory starkly: "The accumulation of all powers, legislative, executive and judiciary, in the same hands...may justly be pronounced the very definition of tyranny."

But there was a second objective, somewhat different from the first: how to assure that the government did not, over time—despite the words of the Constitution—become the tyranny that the Framers feared. This they hoped to avoid by giving each of the branches an opportunity, in pursuing its own interests, to check the powers of the others. The president, for example, can veto legislation enacted by Congress; Congress has the power to confirm the top officers of the executive branch and to appropriate funds for both the executive and the judiciary; and the judiciary can assure that the other branches are staying in their assigned constitutional lanes. In *Federalist* No. 51, Madison again makes the Framers' reasoning clear, describing why a system of checks and balances is necessary even when the branches have separate and exclusive powers:

> To what expedient, then, shall we finally resort, for *maintaining in practice* the necessary partition of power among the several departments, as laid down in the Constitution? The only answer that can be given is, that as all these exterior provisions [i.e., the language of the Constitution] are found to be inadequate, the defect must be supplied, by so contriving the interior structure of the government as that its several constituent parts may, by their mutual relations, be the means of *keeping each other in their proper places.* (Emphasis added)

Madison is telling us that the checks and balances in the Constitution were based on what the Framers conceived were the permanent interests of the three constituent parts of the government; as long as these interests existed, each part would work to limit the abuse of power by the others. If one of the branches moved outside its constitutionally assigned place, the others would have incentives to rein it in. As this book argues, this central idea in the Framers' structure has been lost over time, primarily because of such things as the growth of political parties (discussed in the next chapter) and the idea that the courts should limit their judicial review of administrative rules by deferring to agencies' interpretation of their own authorities.

If we are to be faithful to the constitutional structure as described above, it is necessary to accept the idea that judicial restraint—long a governance principle of conservatives on or off the courts—must be modified in part: "in part" because it is still true, as conservatives have always held, that the courts have no role in public policy and should never impose their views on policy matters. But judicial restraint is not appropriate if it is used or intended to exclude the courts from the role that the Framers intended for them—to determine and declare when either of the other branches steps outside its assigned role under the constitutional separation of powers. Justice Gorsuch made exactly this point concurring in the 2018 case *Sessions v. Dimaya*, where the Court held that a provision of the Immigration and Nationality Act was too vague to be enforced. The ruling, he said, requires Congress only

> to act with enough clarity that reasonable people can know what is required of them and judges can apply the law consistent with their limited office. Our history surely bears examples of the judicial misuse of the so-called "substantive component" of due process to dictate policy on matters that belonged to the people to decide. But concerns with substantive due process should not lead us to react by withdrawing an ancient procedural protection [the vagueness doctrine] compelled by the original meaning of the Constitution.[2]

In the same way, the courts are not abandoning judicial restraint if they enforce the Framers' constitutional structure by declaring that Congress has improperly delegated its legislative authority, or by determining that an agency has exceeded the powers it was properly granted by Congress. As Richard Epstein notes:

> Conservative originalists cannot remain faithful to the twin commitments of fidelity to text on the one hand and judicial restraint on the other. It is therefore a hopeful sign that on many key issues...conservative originalists have begun to move away from the mantra of judicial restraint....The Constitution is written in broad bold strokes, which at some points confer vast powers on government and at others impose major limitations on their exercise.[3]

The Framers Sought to Create a Republic, Not a Popular Democracy

There are occasional arguments about whether the United States—with the restrictions on the federal government in the Constitution—was intended to be a democracy. Madison avoided the issue by defining democracy as a system in which the people directly elect their officials, ruling it out for a large and geographically extended polity like the thirteen original colonies. He called the government formed by the Constitution a republic, and that is the way most of the Framers seemed to have thought of it. Benjamin Franklin, when asked what the Constitutional Convention had created, is said to have replied, "a republic, if you can keep it."

To the Framers, the difference between a republic and a democracy was not a small point. They thought of a democracy as a political form that puts the contemporary will of the people into effect, and this appears to be precisely what the Framers sought to avoid. When they called their structure a republic they meant that—while the people's liberties were protected from restraints imposed by the government—the representatives of the people, and not the people themselves, would make the fundamental decisions. The popular will, while eventually expressed, would first be channeled through a number of circuitous paths that moderated and delayed its effect.

The most obvious of these circuitous paths was the Electoral College, which was the Constitution's method for choosing the president. This body was likely expected to consist of prominent individuals from each state, chosen by popular vote in the manner each state would provide; the number of electors in each state would be equal to the state's representatives in Congress plus its two senators. Under Article II, the electors were to cast their votes for two people; the person who received both a majority of all the electoral votes and the largest number of electoral votes was to be the president, and the person with both a majority and the next largest number of votes was to be the vice president. Since there was no way to narrow the number of potential choices—the Framers had apparently not anticipated the rise of political parties—it was probably assumed that the president and vice president would in most cases actually be elected by Congress in the detailed manner the Constitution described. If this had remained true, the president's constituency would have been a majority in Congress, which would have substantially undercut any claim to a popular mandate.

This structure was substantially changed by the advent of political parties. In the election of 1836, Martin Van Buren—running as a Democrat—won the presidency by choosing a slate of electors in each state pledged to vote for him, and this became the pattern for the future. Although the Electoral College still exists, it is now largely a formality. In most states the winning candidate in the state's presidential election gets all the state's electors. This turns the presidential election into a series of state elections, so that the winning candidate nationally is the one who gets the most electoral votes, not the most popular votes. Five presidents have been elected by winning in the Electoral College while losing the popular vote, including twice in this century, in 2000 and 2016. The Framers' efforts to deny the president a popular majority thus remains at least partially effective, despite the changes wrought by the development of the political party system.

Other provisions that tend to reduce the democratic nature of the American government include the creation of two houses of Congress, one of which—the House of Representatives—was to be made up of popularly elected representatives from each state. Although the Constitution does not require districts, the states have chosen to elect their representatives by district rather than at large; technically, then, and often in reality, the members of Congress represent their districts, not even their states, making it difficult to assemble a popular majority in favor of any policy. The other house—the Senate—was to consist of two senators from each state chosen by the state legislature. This procedure was changed by the Seventeenth Amendment, which required senators to be popularly elected in each state. Still, senators are elected for six years, while representatives are elected for two, and senators' terms are staggered so that only one-third of the Senate is elected in each even-numbered year. These restrictions, too, were obviously intended to mediate the "passions" of the people by making it difficult for a popular majority to capture the elected branches in a single election.

Somewhat surprisingly, the Framers advertised the limited role they expected the public to play in the major decisions of the government. For example, in *Federalist* No. 63, thought to have been written by either Hamilton or Madison, the pseudonymous Publius says that "the true distinction" between the government structure envisioned in the proposed constitution and the governments of ancient Rome and Greece "lies *in the total exclusion of the people, in their collective capacity*" (emphasis in the original) from any role in the administration of the government. The government was to be carried on by the people's representatives, not by the people themselves.

The extraordinary fact is that the Constitution, with these antimajoritarian elements, was heavily debated in each state—the *Federalist Papers* were written as the Framers' side of the debate—and won majorities in all. So there can be little doubt that the Framers' plan for restricting and restraining a majoritarian system was understood by the individual state populations that ultimately approved the new Constitution. "Generally," as the constitutional scholar Walter Berns summarizes it, "the Constitution provides a system of majority government, but the governing majority is assembled not from among the people directly but from among the representatives of the people."[4] And even more explicitly:

> The men who founded this country surely recognized the entitlements of a popular majority, but, with an eye to the qualifications for or the qualities required of an office, they devised institutions— the electoral college was one of them—that modify or qualify the majority principle. Nothing could be clearer than that the Founders sought institutions or ways—Alexis de Tocqueville called them "forms"—that would protect the country from what has come to be called populism.[5]

Again, the Framers' ultimate objective appears to have been to place obstacles in the way of temporary populist majorities that—on the basis of what the Framers called "passions"—might threaten the liberties of all.

The Judiciary's Role in the Separation of Powers

Although the courts' function in the separation of powers and the checks and balances system is not laid out in detail in Article III of the Constitution, it is clear that the courts were seen by the Framers as "guardians" of the Constitution's structure and thus important protectors of liberty. As noted in the introduction, Hamilton refers to the judiciary in just these terms in *Federalist* No. 78, and argues that the Framers granted judges lifetime appointments to shield them from the pressures of the elected branches. The obvious purpose, as Hamilton notes, is to give the courts the "fortitude" to disagree with and possibly overturn acts of the political branches.

Article III of the Constitution states: "The judicial Power shall extend to all Cases, in Law and Equity, arising under this Constitution, the Laws of the United States, and Treaties made, or which shall be made, under their Authority…" Filling out the meaning of this clause in the famous 1803 case *Marbury v. Madison*, Chief Justice John Marshall not only established the logical principle that the judiciary can declare laws unconstitutional, he also said that, "It is emphatically the province and duty of the Judicial Department to say what the law is. Those who apply the rule to particular cases must, of necessity, expound and interpret that rule."[6] What this certainly means is that the courts have a responsibility to interpret the laws, not only to determine their constitutionality but also to decide what authority the laws confer on the president and the president's administration.

Logically, then, the courts must interpret the laws passed by Congress as Congress intended at the time they were passed, not as the executive chooses to interpret them afterward. If the executive can interpret the laws as it wishes, the powers of Congress are substantially reduced, violating the principles underlying both the separation of powers and the related idea of checks and balances. Writing in the early years of the republic, Chief Justice Marshall seems clearly to have seen the powers of the judiciary in this light. As discussed in chapter 1, in several instances administrative agencies have adopted expansive interpretations of laws enacted by Congress that were readily accepted by the courts. There is no way of knowing whether these interpretations were in the collective mind of Congress when the laws were passed, but we do know that when a law is enacted it has often been through an arduous process of political compromise. An administrative agency's interpretation of what Congress meant by the legislative language it adopted may be biased by the agency's desire to expand its power or increase its appropriations. It is up to the courts—in the structure conceived by the Framers—to say what Congress meant. It is also the only way to obtain an unbiased assessment of that question.

Similarly, as Justice Gorsuch observed in his *Dimaya* concurrence, it would also be a violation of the separation of powers if the courts were to go beyond what Congress intended in interpreting a statute. That, too, would be usurping the exclusive legislative authority of Congress:

> Under the Constitution, the adoption of new laws restricting liberty is supposed to be a hard business, the product of an open and public debate among a large and diverse number of elected representatives. Allowing the legislature to hand off the job of lawmaking risks substituting this design for one where legislation is made easy, with a mere handful of unelected judges and prosecutors free to "condem[n] all that [they] personally disapprove and for no better reason than [they] disapprove it."[7]

The Separation of Powers and the "Modern, Complex Economy"

To justify and explain the growth of the administrative state, many commentators assert that there is little alternative to the powerful administrative agencies we have today. The U.S. economy is too complex, it is argued, and Congress and the courts are insufficiently expert, to restrict the scope of administrative rulemaking. The preceding chapter on regulation and the rule of law challenges this idea. If administrative agencies can—with the approval of the courts—interpret the laws that Congress has enacted in any way the agencies wish, how is this different from what Madison described as the "very definition of tyranny"? All the powers of government, in this case, are in the same hands. Even conceding that there are cases where the expertise of administrative agencies is needed, where do the rules of administrative agencies gain their legitimacy if not from the faithful execution of the laws made by Congress? The fact that administrative rules are obeyed today does not mean they will always be regarded as legitimate. Brexit tells us that. At some point, people who have become accustomed to having some control over their government will move to regain it.

Looking again at administrative actions such as Operation Choke Point, how can anyone be confident that giving administrative agencies the latitude they want will ultimately preserve the American people's liberties? Both the Obama Justice Department and its collaborating bank regulators claimed to have lawful authority to close down bank financing of payday lenders and others, even though there was nothing in the laws they were purporting to enforce that gave them the authority to drive otherwise lawful activities out of business. Eventually, the D.C. Federal District Court found that the Justice Department and the agencies had acted unlawfully. Can we really feel comfortable giving unrestricted authority to people who act this way, simply because we live in a complex society? If we really have to choose, as some imply, between a government that is not fully competent to deal with a complex society and a government that will disregard any restrictions on its authority in order to achieve some ideological goal, we must necessarily choose (or settle for) the former.

It is also significant, in terms of the Framers' structure, that in the case of Operation Choke Point it was the judiciary that stepped in to stop an outlaw action by government. As noted earlier, if the federal district court judge who heard the challenge to the program had not been appointed for life and thus been made independent of the power of a sitting president and his principal legal arm, the outcome of the case could have set a precedent for more lawlessness rather than the termination of it. As this example shows, the independence of the branches of our government, one from another, with different roles to play in creating and enforcing the laws, is as essential today in this so-called complex economy as it was when Madison framed the issue for the voters of the state of New York in *Federalist* No. 47.

It might be argued, of course, that the Choke Point initiative was unusual, an outlier that should not be used to justify the continuation of the separation of powers or the related idea of checks and balances. But in other examples reviewed in chapter 1, government agencies also appear to have acted without obvious support in statutory law. The Department of Education and its predecessor had pressed upon the courts that a statute (Title IX of the Education Amendments of 1972) that says a person cannot be deprived of "educational resources" on account of that person's sex can be used to forbid one student from making a statement that another student finds offensive. Is it reasonable to believe that this is what Congress meant when it enacted Title IX? By approving this interpretation, the courts gave the Education Department the latitude to go even further: to specify how a person who is charged with making an offensive statement should be tried and punished. Similarly, the Supreme Court itself upheld the disparate impact theory as HUD applied it in the context of the Fair Housing Act, even though the act itself—or the Civil Rights Act of 1964 on which it is based—says nothing about disparate impact.

In these examples, agencies developed rules that were, at best, interpolations from language in a congressionally enacted law, and in both examples the courts endorsed the theories that the agencies advanced. This was clearly a failure of the separation of powers as the Framers conceived it. In the Choke Point case, Congress had given bank regulators limited authority to make sure banks were operating safely, but the agencies did not act as though the authority was limited. Instead, they treated the language as a starting point for what they were permitted to do, and spun it out as far as they wished because—as covered in the chapter on *Chevron* deference—the courts have been directed to defer to an agency's interpretation of what Congress enacted. Operation Choke Point was egregious, to be sure, but it was only one example among many in which administrative agencies have used laws in ways Congress did not intend. Such uses are only possible if the judiciary surrenders its constitutional responsibility to interpret the law. It also demonstrates, once again, that Madison was right: the separation of powers is necessary to preserve the liberties of the American people. But each of the three branches must play its role. Up to now, and certainly since *Chevron*, that has not been uniformly true of the judicial branch.

Unfortunately, *Chevron* is not the only precedent for ignoring the compromises reached in the legislative process. Examples abound, but one worth discussing further is Justice Breyer's dissent in *Utility Air*, with which three other justices concurred.

That dissent, described earlier, was notable for its emphasis on the *purpose* of a statute, not its specific language. According to the dissent, the Court should have put itself in the place of Congress, and asked what Congress would have decided if it had been confronted with the fact that CO_2 could be considered a pollutant.[8] This seems a misuse of an inquiry into the purpose of a statute. Courts frequently look to a law's purpose in order to get a clearer understanding of what its words were supposed to mean, but here Justice Breyer is implying that a court can use the law's purpose to disregard its actual words. His dissent is a direct challenge to the separation of powers because it takes from Congress the opportunity to settle an issue by enacting a law. Whatever words Congress might ultimately adopt in the course of debate and compromise could be disregarded by the executive if it concludes that Congress's actual purpose was something other than was expressed in its words.

Indeed, interpreting a statute according to its perceived purpose is the very opposite of judicial restraint, because it provides the courts with an open field for justifying their own policy preferences, as Justice Breyer's dissent in *Utility Air* clearly shows. It is also impossible for a diligent judge to know such a thing, as Judge Frank H. Easterbrook made clear in a widely cited 1983 article on statutory interpretation:

> Few of the best-intentioned, most humble, and most restrained among us have the skills necessary to learn the temper of time before our births, to assume the identity of people we have never met, and to know how 535 disparate characters from regions of great political and economic diversity would have answered questions that never occurred to them.... After putting the impossible to one side, though, a judge must choose from among the possible solutions, and here human ingenuity is bound to fail, often. When it fails, even the best intentioned will find that the imagined dialogues of departed legislators have much in common with their own conceptions of the good.[9]

The dissent, however, went even further on this point than allowing courts to put statutory purpose over statutory words. Justice Breyer continued: "The EPA, exercising the legal authority to which it is entitled under *Chevron*..., understood the [250-ton] threshold's purpose in the same light. It explained that Congress's objective was 'to limit the [act's effect] to large industrial sources because it was those sources that were the primary cause of the pollution problems in question and because those sources would have the resources to comply with the [act's] requirements.'"[10] Accordingly, four members of the Court would have extended *Chevron* to allow an administrative agency to consider the purpose of a statute in issuing a rule, even if the rule violates the actual words of the statute.

This is far more troubling than giving that power to the courts. It would allow agencies to go beyond what Congress—often after much debate and compromise—actually voted on. It is difficult enough, although legitimate, for a court to determine what Congress intended by a statute, and thus to determine "what the law is." But to allow administrative agencies to disregard the words of a statute, in order to achieve the agencies' idea of what Congress intended, is a bridge too far. For one thing, the agency is not an objective observer; its view of Congress's purpose is biased by its interest in extending its own power. In addition, since individuals have to adjust their behavior to comply with both the regulations and the underlying law, a knowledge of the statutory language will not be a useful guide to what regulations the agency might adopt. No lawyer can tell his client what is permitted under a statute if an administrative agency can make rules based on what it believes Congress *intended* by the law rather than what Congress actually said.

Thus the dissent's willingness to allow administrative agencies, under *Chevron*, to use statutory purpose in interpreting the scope of their authorities would not only challenge the separation of powers but also seriously impair the rule of law. As Madison presciently recognizes in *Federalist* No. 62:

> What prudent merchant will hazard his fortunes in any new branch of commerce when he knows not but that his plans may be rendered unlawful before they can be executed? What farmer or manufacturer will lay himself out for the encouragement given to any particular cultivation or establishment, when he can have no assurance that his preparatory labors and advances will not render him a victim to an inconstant government?

Checks and Balances

Although occasionally called the fourth branch of government, administrative agencies are very much part of the executive branch. Even the independent agencies, multiheaded, bipartisan bodies that used to be called "arms of Congress," are now no longer considered outside the president's control. In the Dodd-Frank Act, for example, Congress required the heads of all the independent regulatory agencies to become part of the Financial Stability Oversight Council, where they function under the chairmanship of the secretary of the Treasury, one of the principal political and policy officers of any administration. The question, however, is not whether administrative agencies belong to the executive branch, but whether they are free of the constraints that the Framers thought they were putting in place when they created a government based on a separation of powers.

In *Federalist* No. 51, cited earlier, Madison argues that checks and balances are necessary to keep the separation of powers from deteriorating over time—leaving the people's liberties in jeopardy. In the same document, Madison describes why and how the separation of powers would work:

> [T]he great security against a gradual concentration of the several powers in the same department, consists in giving to those who administer each department the necessary constitutional means and *personal motives* to resist encroachments of the others.... *Ambition must be made to counteract ambition....* In framing a government which is to be administered by men over men, the great difficulty lies in this: you must first enable the government to control the governed; and in the next place oblige it to control itself. (Emphasis added)

Thus, a key element of the Framers' plan was to rely on the rivalrous tendencies of human beings —the competing ambitions and jealousies of the president, Congress, and the courts—to keep the government as a whole from becoming too powerful. The Framers expected that if each of the branches had its own responsibilities and powers, it would act to keep the others out of its domain, except as the Constitution itself required them to share responsibilities. In chapter 3, on Congress, we will see that this theory has not worked as the Framers planned, principally because of the rise of political parties. Unanticipated by the Framers, the advent of political parties brings Congress and the president into alignment when both are controlled by the same political party.

If the original system had worked as planned, the legislation Congress enacts would be narrowly drawn to avoid handing too much discretionary authority to the president and the agencies of the executive branch. The courts, in turn, would have incentives to construe statutes narrowly, lest their interpretations be overturned by a Congress jealous of its powers. Although this is how the system was supposed to work, it is not how it works today. Since the Progressive Era, and especially since the New Deal—both discussed in chapter 4—the judiciary has been markedly reluctant to impose restraints on the agencies of the executive branch. In *Chevron*, decided in 1984, this reluctance has been formalized into deference—a willingness, not expected by the Framers, to accept the executive's interpretation of the statutory language on which its authorities rest. That is how Title IX of the 1972 Education Act Amendments was distorted into something Congress could not have imagined when it adopted the language, and how other administrative actions that seem to exceed what Congress authorized have come into effect.

This judicial stance is wrongly conceived, and ignores the responsibilities of the judiciary in the checks and balances system the Framers devised. The legislative process is complicated. Congress starts with committee hearings. Then a draft of legislation is "marked up" by the committee of jurisdiction, with votes on every disputed provision; if it passes out of the committee, it goes to the floor, where it is often amended again. If the bill passes the House, it goes to the Senate, and vice versa. If the two houses disagree, a conference committee tries to find common ground, and if that effort is successful the conference version goes to both chambers for a final vote. This process tends to promote compromises on policy that are reflected in the language in the bill. When the president signs the bill, that language becomes the law.

Obviously, in the history of American governance, Congress has done a lot of work to find legislative language that can gain acceptance from a majority of both chambers. Where in this process is there license for today's administrative agencies to read their own interpretation into the statutory language, let alone the *Chevron* idea that where Congress has been *silent* on an issue the administrative agency is implicitly authorized to make a binding rule that covers the point? Although Congress has labored to produce the words on which majorities in both the House and Senate could agree, executive agencies, with the deference of the courts, can and do read into the legislative language policy positions Congress may never have considered, or may even have rejected somewhere during the long legislative process.

In reviewing the courts' willingness to enlarge Title IX and insert the disparate impact theory into the Fair Housing Act, we see little of the countervailing ambition that Madison was counting on to prevent one branch of government from gathering too much power into its own hands. Certainly, the personal motives of the members of the administrative bureaucracy are clear—their motives are consistent with the enhancement of their power—but we do not see Congress defending itself, or the courts reading what Congress has done in a way that sets any boundaries on the actions of these agencies. Instead, in the case of disparate impact, we see the Supreme Court allowing an agency to read into a statute something that Congress did not include in the legislative language and may never have considered.

As early as 1927, in a much simpler time, Felix Frankfurter, a devoted Progressive but not yet a justice of the Supreme Court, was pleased that administrative agencies were already building up a "body of law not written by legislatures":

> Hardly a measure passes Congress the effective execution of which is not conditioned upon rules and regulations emanating from the enforcing authorities. These administrative complements are euphemistically called "filling in the details" of a policy set forth in statutes. But the "details" are of the essence; they give meaning and content to vague contours. The control of banking, insurance, public utilities, finance, industry, the professions, health and morals, in sum, the manifold response of government to the forces and needs of modern society, is building up a body of laws not written by legislatures, and of adjudications not made by courts and not subject to their revision.[11]

Later, as the growth of administrative agencies and the effect of their interpretations of statute became clearer, growing concerns were expressed in the legal community and elsewhere. Walter Gellhorn, one of the giants of administrative law, tried to reassure those who were fearful of the effect of administrative interpretations on the separation of powers. "We have seen," he wrote, "that delegation is necessary if regulation is to exist in the form of other than broadly stated principles; and *we have discovered that so long as the representative legislature remains supreme—so long as it can modify or repeal rules the executive has made pursuant to delegated authority—the danger of tyranny is not overwhelming.*"[12] Gellhorn wrote this underwhelming justification of administrative activity in 1941, when the administrative state was just beginning its run; one wonders how he would assess the possibility of "tyranny" today.

In the next chapter, on Congress, we will see that, today, the legislative branch—which the Framers thought would be the most powerful—has been reduced to the weakest, and in chapters 6 and 7 we will see that the judiciary, by abandoning to administrative agencies the courts' role as interpreters of the meaning of Congress's statutory language, has been the principal agent in this massive reordering of power within the constitutional system. Put another way, when the judiciary stopped reading the words in statutes as limitations on the discretion available to administrative agencies, a critical balance wheel in the allocation of power between Congress and the executive was removed, reducing the role and power of Congress.

There are indications now that the freedom the courts have provided to administrative agencies has created a powerful and unaccountable bureaucracy, which is gradually supplanting Congress as a policy-making body. As a result, the United States today seems less like a constitutional republic in which the people's representatives decide the rules, and more like a benevolent dictatorship consisting of an unaccountable special class that makes the rules for everyone else. Restoring the balance envisioned by the Framers—returning Congress to at least a semblance of its former position and reining in the administrative state—is possible. It requires only that the judiciary step up to its original responsibilities in the constitutional structure.

3

CONGRESS AND THE ADMINISTRATIVE STATE

The [Founding] Fathers were of course right in predicting, as Gouverneur Morris did, that the "critical moments produced by war, invasion, or convulsion" would be seized for the aggrandizement of governmental power; but they mistook the branch of government that would do the seizing.

JAMES BURNHAM, *CONGRESS AND THE AMERICAN TRADITION*

Although it is difficult to imagine now, the Framers thought Congress would be so dominant within the system they had devised that it would be difficult to control its inherent power. As James Burnham writes, "Granted the maintenance of a firmly republican system, the Fathers anticipated little danger of executive tyranny and none at all of judicial. The constitutional problem was, rather, to devise a structure wherein the executive and judiciary would not be altogether swallowed up by the legislative branch."[1]

As described more fully in chapter 2, the Framers tried to solve this problem by adopting a checks and balances system. The president could veto legislation, but his veto could be overridden; the judiciary would interpret the law, and judges were appointed for life; the Congress could impeach both the president and the judges, but Congress itself would be divided between two houses, one of which would represent the people based on population while the other would represent the states.

For more than a hundred years, this structure worked. It was stressed during the Civil War, to be sure, with the presidency assuming new powers through Lincoln's use of his authority as commander in chief of the armed forces, but after the war it returned to roughly the prior system. Indeed, Woodrow Wilson, writing in 1884, complains bitterly and sarcastically about the power of Congress: "The checks and balances which once obtained are no longer effective.... We are really living under a constitution essentially different from that which we have been so long worshiping as our own peculiar and incomparable possession.... The actual form of our present government is simply a scheme of congressional supremacy."[2] Ironically, Wilson also saw the judiciary as the only constitutional mechanism that could tame the Congress, just as today the judiciary appears to be the only mechanism that can bring the executive back within the constitutional framework: "The legislature is the aggressive spirit," Wilson goes on. "It is the motive power of the government, and unless the judiciary can check it, the courts are of comparatively little worth as balance-wheels in the system."[3]

The dominance of Congress was substantially eroded during the Progressive Era (see chapter 4), especially with the election of Wilson in 1912, but it was essentially ended during the presidency of Franklin Roosevelt, when the Democratic Congress became a trusted rubber stamp for the president's New Deal proposals. It has never recovered. So far had Congress fallen by midcentury that Burnham, a conservative favorable to a Congress able to hold its own in the constitutional structure, could write in 1959:

> The coarse fact about the position of Congress in the American political system is simple enough: Congress once held a large, quite probably the largest, share in the total sum of power possessed by the central government; and now it holds a share that is not merely smaller but so much smaller as to be of a different order of magnitude. This is equivalent to saying that in the American governmental system a constitutional revolution has taken place, through which Congress has been reduced from a coordinate or predominate to a secondary and subordinate rank.[4]

The decline in the importance of Congress is traceable to the development of political parties, something that the Framers appear not to have considered. Indeed, in *Federalist* No. 10, Madison seemed to denounce political parties as factions, "adversed to the rights of other citizens, or to the permanent and aggregate interests of the community." His remedy was a large republic, in which he thought factions were unlikely to become dominant. This was, for Madison, a remarkably obtuse and unrealistic misreading of human nature, and it gave way quickly when political parties began to organize shortly after the government was formed. Because the Constitution failed to take account of how political parties would operate, several of its major elements did not function as expected.

The first to go was one of the key elements of the Framers' structure, the Electoral College. This was seen by the Framers as a mediating device that would cool populist sentiments as they might erupt in a presidential election. Voters were to vote for electors—presumably prominent and sensible individuals—who, in turn, would cast their votes for the person they thought would be the best president. But in the election of 1836, Martin Van Buren in effect amended the Constitution by organizing slates of electors made up of members of the Democratic Party pledged to vote for him for president. As Gerald Leonard notes in an article about Van Buren,

> most of us have not been taught to think of Van Buren's election as especially significant, let alone constitutionally transformative. But Van Buren's success in 1836 reflected a profound and permanent alteration of the American constitutional order, because he was elected not as the champion of some set of policy positions but—in defiance of the Madisonian constitutional design—as the candidate of a mass political party. Even more importantly, he was elected as the champion of the idea of party itself as the new organizing principle of a states' rights Constitution.[5]

The effect of this change on the separation of powers was profound, and was probably not recognized at the time it occurred, or even today. As noted earlier, it's likely that the Framers believed that most presidential elections would be decided in the House of Representatives, reducing the president's ability to develop a political base. After 1836, election by the

House became highly unlikely and, even more important, every elected president had a political base from which he could challenge the power of Congress.

The Role of Political Parties in the Weakening of Congress

Nevertheless, as Wilson ruefully noted, through the rest of the nineteenth century Congress remained the dominant force in the American political system. It continued as such through much of the twentieth century; House members and senators had independent political bases that allowed or encouraged them to act independently of the president. The political party system, like the nation itself, was more fragmented than it is today. While members of the president's party in the House and Senate certainly tended to look favorably on his policies, the prerogatives of Congress as a whole—as the Framers had intended—exerted a greater pull on their loyalties; they could not always be counted on to follow the president's lead. Even in the 1930s, when the Democratic Party controlled Congress with overwhelming majorities, and FDR got most of what he wanted from Congress in short order, there were a few occasions—such as the president's proposal to "pack" the Supreme Court—when Congress refused to go along.

But the trend was clear. After the New Deal, the president was a more dominant figure than before, and he commanded a government of agencies that also had considerably more power over economic decisions. More important, when both houses of Congress were held by the same party, Congress was much more willing to provide broad legislative authorities to the president, and to agencies in the executive branch. One prominent example was the willingness of the Democratic Congress, after the assassination of President John F. Kennedy and the landslide election of Lyndon Johnson in 1964, to enact broadly worded legislation providing significant new powers to the executive that went well beyond the New Deal. The War on Poverty, Medicare, and the Civil Rights Act are examples. Similarly, the Democratic Congress elected in 2008, after the financial crisis, enacted the Affordable Care Act and the Dodd-Frank Act, both far-reaching pieces of legislation that gave extraordinary new powers to the executive. Conversely, history shows that when at least one congressional chamber is controlled by the party that does not control the White House the legislation enacted is significantly less open-handed for the executive and its agencies.

The scholars Daryl Levinson and Richard Pildes, citing the work of John Aldrich on American political parties, note that, "from the late 1950s through 1992, the President's own party in Congress voted in favor of legislation he supported almost three-quarters of the time; the opposing party supported him half of the time or less."[6] According to the authors, during periods of unified government—when the same party holds the presidency and both houses of Congress—presidents hardly use their veto power. During times of divided government, Congress is unwilling to give greater discretion to administrative agencies. Citing several empirical studies, the authors note

> that Congress not only delegates significantly less authority to the executive branch during periods of divided government, but also further limits the discretion of executive agencies by binding them with more restrictive procedural constraints. Congress's reluctance to delegate to an opposition-controlled executive branch means that agreement on statutory details must be hammered out up front, which should make it all the more difficult to pass ambitious, controversial legislation. And the agencies charged with administering the enacted statutes are less able to regulate ambitiously or effectively.... Immodest legislative programs like the New Deal and Great Society cannot exist without a Congress willing to delegate to a bureaucracy with broad policymaking discretion.[7]

All this suggests that, at least since the New Deal, party loyalties in Congress have easily overcome the Framers' assumption that Congress would be independent of the president, and vice versa.

This means two things. First, Congress is not a reliable entity for holding the presidency to account. When the president and Congress are controlled by the same party, the rivalry that Madison expected simply does not occur. In fact, in this case Congress enhances the power of the president and the agencies of the executive branch. Second, because regulatory expansion tends to occur in periods when Democrats control both the presidency and the Congress—as with the New Deal and Great Society—this trend has a "ratchet" effect: the administrative state gets significantly more discretion when the Democrats control both the presidency and Congress than when the Republicans do, and this discretion is seldom taken back.

In theory, of course, when Republicans return to power, they can repeal the legislation enacted by the Democrats—but this almost never happens. The reason is that constituencies form around the legislation that has already passed and these groups object strenuously to repeal, raising the political stakes for Congress to attempt repeal. The failure of the Republican Congress in 2017 to repeal the Affordable Care Act (ACA), which was enacted during the Obama administration—despite several years of promising to do so if they were given control of Congress and the presidency—is a clear illustration of this phenomenon. By 2017, insurance companies, state governors, hospitals, Medicaid recipients, and many others who directly or indirectly benefited from the ACA had formed a powerful constituency group in support of the law that the Republicans could not overcome.

Misplaced Confidence in Congress

Accordingly, although many conservatives put their faith in Congress to take back authority it has granted, this is unrealistic. The theory of checks and balances assumes that Congress will jealously guard its legislative authority, but the rise of political parties—and tightening party loyalties since the New Deal—have made this possibility remote. If there is to be any control over the growth of the agencies of the administrative state, it will have to be done through judicial review and not through the political process. There is, as I have argued earlier, nothing illegitimate about this. The Framers clearly understood and expected that the judiciary—if only as a last resort—would keep the political branches within their assigned channels, and if Congress is unable to perform that function for itself the judiciary should step in.

In addition, although Congress has enacted legislation that would enable it to review and repeal regulations that it disapproves, this is seldom done. For example, in 1996 the Republican Congress adopted the Congressional Review Act (CRA), which permits Congress to overturn rules adopted by administrative agencies. The act contains "fast track" elements that allow resolutions to avoid obstacles such as filibusters in the Senate. However, until the Trump administration took office, the act had received very little use, even though the number of these regulations often exceeds three thousand each year. The Congressional Research Service reported in November 2016: "Of the approximately 72,000 final rules that have been submitted to Congress since the [CRA] was enacted in 1996, the CRA has been used to disapprove one rule: the Occupational Safety and Health Administration's November 2000 final rule on ergonomics."[8] That rule, significantly, was promulgated at the end of the Clinton administration and was annulled by a Republican Congress at the outset of the George W. Bush administration.

To be sure, the CRA has limitations. It is applicable only to regulations that were finalized within sixty legislative days of the CRA vote, and the president in office is likely to veto any regulation that was issued during his administration. Nevertheless, what happened at the beginning of the Trump administration indicates that Congress has difficulty mustering the votes to overturn regulations, even in favorable circumstances. In early 2017, shortly after President Trump took office, there was a large number of Obama-issued regulations that were eligible for CRA treatment. Virtually all were what some might call "midnight rules": they were hurriedly issued during the closing days of Obama's term and after it had become clear that Hillary Clinton, the Democratic candidate, was not going to be his successor. In all, there were resolutions introduced in the House of Representatives to overturn nearly three dozen of these rules, and sixteen introduced in the Senate. Ultimately, eighteen resolutions cleared both houses and were signed by President Trump. In addition, there was an unknown number of rules that could have been repealed because the agencies that issued them had neglected to take the necessary step of filing the rule with Congress. These rules were therefore indefinitely eligible for repeal, but none were brought up during the period when Congress actually had the necessary time to consider and vote on them.

It may seem a bit churlish to question this record, which resulted in the elimination of many expensive and unnecessary regulations, but the circumstances for use of the CRA could not have been more favorable than in early 2017. The Republicans controlled both houses of Congress, and the new president then in office had made deregulation one of the principal themes of his campaign. Moreover, a new Congress had just been seated; there were no other legislative priorities on the table. Nevertheless, even under the expedited procedures in place, Congress could only muster the votes to send eighteen CRA resolutions to the president.

At the beginning of the 115th Congress, in January 2017, a number of new legislative proposals intended to provide Congress with opportunities to overturn regulations were introduced, or in some cases reintroduced, in the House of Representatives. These include the REINS (Regulations from the Executive in Need of Scrutiny) Act, which would require "major" rules to be referred to Congress for fast-track approval or disapproval, the Midnight Rule Relief Act, and the Regulatory Accountability Act, all three of which ultimately passed the House but were never acted on in the Senate. Other bills were introduced but received no action. The sheer number of proposals reflects the frustration in Congress about its inability to stanch the flow of regulations. But the failure of Congress so far to get these ameliorative laws through both houses and to the president's desk suggests how difficult it would be to use any of them, even if passed.

The fact that there has been no action on any of these bills in the Senate is further evidence that Congress is not able effectively to address the growth of the administrative state. The easiest part of reining in the administrative agencies is passing the legislation to do so. It is not difficult to stir opposition to future rules and regulations. The difficult part is taking concerted action to overturn regulations when they have actually been issued and already attracted constituencies that support them.

Finally, it is doubtful that laws like this will actually be effective in overturning regulations that have already been issued. As Christopher DeMuth, who served as director of the Office of Information and Regulatory Affairs during the Reagan administration, writes about the REINS Act:

A dozen or more times every year (depending on the definition of "major" rules), members would be obliged to vote for or against costly, often controversial, sometimes excruciatingly detailed rules rather than cheering or booing from the sidelines.... REINS-approved rules would be statutory law, and therefore immune to [Administrative Procedure Act] judicial review (the proposal has so far been drafted to preserve APA review, but no court would reject on other than constitutional grounds a rule enacted by Congress and president). As the agencies became adept at crafting REINS-worthy rules, they could use them to secure de facto statutory revisions that expanded their jurisdiction.[9]

It is odd that so many academic analysts continue to argue that Congress is actually in control of the administrative state, when in fact the evidence—presented in this chapter and elsewhere in this book—runs quite the other way. [10] Courts may also be under this mistaken impression, causing them to consider that Congress intended broader authority for agencies than in fact it had.

However, the inability of Congress to enact laws that restrain the growth of the administrative state, despite many efforts, is simply one example of Congress's difficulty with enacting controversial laws in general. This has always been true, but it has become a lot harder and less rewarding as the courts, under the influence of the *Chevron* case, have withdrawn much of their interest in reviewing administrative interpretations of statutes and the Supreme Court (as discussed in chapter 6) has refused to entertain a serious claim of unconstitutional delegation of legislative authority.

Chevron Further Weakens Congress

As discussed elsewhere in this book, legislation is a time-consuming and difficult process, which involves hearings, markups of draft legislation, compromise on language, and eventually a vote for or against a legislative proposal. It is far easier if the proposal simply states a goal, without disappointing one set of interests and favoring another, creating an incentive in Congress to enact legislation that merely passes the responsibility to an administrative agency rather than fighting over legislative language. Accordingly, unless Congress is compelled by the courts to make controversial decisions, its preferred position will be to adopt a goal such as clean air or clean water and leave it to the administrative agency to determine what that is, what it requires of the public and businesses, and who ultimately bears the costs.

According to DeMuth's summary of the creation of the Occupational Safety and Health Administration, this is exactly what happened:

> Congress was clearly going to establish a new agency to promote occupational health and safety through rules and standards, but key legislators were at odds over the criteria for agency standard-setting. Rather than compromising among preferences for more- and less-stringent criteria, they threw all of them in—combining an absolute-sounding, no-employee-left-behind goal with several prudential qualifications, to indeterminate effect. That gave every member something to crow about and left the actual policymaking to the new agency.[11]

The inevitable result was the 1980 Supreme Court decision in *Industrial Union Department, AFL-CIO v. American Petroleum Institute.*[12] Four justices thought the Secretary of Labor had not complied with the broad language of the law ("reasonable" and "feasible" were the key words) that had authorized the secretary to limit the use of benzene in the workplace; four justices thought he had complied; and one, Justice William Rehnquist, concurred in sending the case back to the Labor Department because he thought the statute contained an unconstitutional delegation of legislative authority.

As noted in chapter 6, enacting laws that require administrative agencies to make the major policy decisions in administering a law *should* be seen by the courts as an unconstitutional delegation of legislative authority. It is not even sensible legislative policy for Congress to delegate wide discretion to an administrative agency. Doing so opens issues for litigation that could not be challenged (except on a constitutional basis) if decided by Congress itself. The very essence of legislation, after all, is the arbitrary and discretionary power to make the difficult choices that favor one group of interests over another. Everything after those choices are made is justifiably considered administration.

Unfortunately, as discussed in chapter 7, *Chevron* actually encourages this behavior by Congress. There, a unanimous Court concluded that when a policy choice has not been made by Congress—that is, Congress has left an ambiguity in the law—the administrative agency's decision in filling that space must be respected by the courts if it is "reasonable." So Congress is encouraged to follow the course of least resistance and enact ambiguous or policy-free legislation that will move the tough decisions in the legislative process to the bureaucracies of the administrative state, while Congress takes a bow for "solving" a politically difficult problem.

A good example of ambiguous legislation is provided by the Telecommunications Act of 1996. There, the Federal Communications Commission (FCC) was directed "to enhance, to the extent technically feasible and economically reasonable, access to advanced telecommunications and information services for all public and nonprofit elementary and secondary school classrooms, health care providers, and libraries."[13] Every part of this provision, jointly sponsored by four Senate Republicans and Democrats, is an example of a goal-oriented law in which Congress avoided any real decision; it was left to the FCC to decide what was "technically feasible" and "economically reasonable," though it was obvious that these decisions would require communications firms to provide costly resources to favored groups. How costly it would be—the crux of the section—was left to the administrative agency.

Litigation ultimately developed about "access to advanced telecommunications and information services." It was not clear whether "access" meant running wires to a building or doing the internal wiring, and whether, if internal wiring was required, it meant every classroom and also included training and support for the teaching and custodial staff. Naturally, the recipients of the services wanted everything they could get, and in the Clinton administration that is what the FCC decided the language meant. The telecom firms sued, and the Fifth Circuit Court of

Appeals found that the language was ambiguous, so that under *Chevron* the FCC's choice merely had to be reasonable—which the court found it was.[14]

Does Congress Want to Protect Its Prerogatives?

The question, then, is how the administrative state will ever be brought under control if Congress is encouraged—as it was in the benzene and FCC cases—to legislate a benefit without having to define it in any detail, leaving it to the administrative agency to decide who pays for the benefit and how much. Similarly, the lesson Congress would undoubtedly draw from the FCC case is that its members can earn a lot of credit from the groups who benefit from an ambiguous law, with no political price. Even if the companies—or more likely their shareholders—were angry enough to reproach the members of Congress who voted for this bill, the reaction would be utterly predictable: "I'm sorry that the decision was made that way by the FCC, but that is not what I voted for."

In a paper presented at a Hoover Institution conference in June 2016, former appellate court judge Michael W. McConnell summarized this problem well: "Congress delegates power to the executive because that is the most politically convenient way to achieve its objectives.... Delegation of standardless discretion allows Congress to pretend to address problems—even when it has no clue—and then, as a bonus, to complain if the executive's solution turns out to pinch important constituent (or donor) groups."[15] Our government is not supposed to operate this way, but it is the logical consequence of the way the Supreme Court has structured Congress's incentives.

There are other adverse outcomes in Congress that are natural consequences of allowing the administrative state to take over policy making. Knowing that an administrative agency—in a liberal administration—is likely to make the kind of decision that the FCC made in the case concerning the Telecommunications Act, a liberal policy entrepreneur in Congress who wanted that outcome could explicitly urge that the statute be kept ambiguous. This would further the likelihood of its enactment, and the outcome for the liberal legislator would be exactly what he wanted. He might even know beforehand what position the agency would take on the ambiguous language. Similarly, a conservative policy entrepreneur adopting legislation that would be administered in a conservative administration would do the same, assuming that the administrative decision would be the outcome he would prefer. In other words, the *Chevron* case encourages Congress to game the system rather than discharge its constitutional responsibilities.

Neomi Rao outlines the problem this creates for the checks and balances system: "Because members can realize individual benefits from influencing delegated authority, their interests will often be misaligned, and sometimes directly at odds, with Congress as an institution. This dynamic erodes what courts and commentators assume will be the primary structural check on delegations—Congress's jealous protection of its lawmaking power."[16] In reality, the incentives for Congress to protect its power all point the wrong way. Members can get credit for legislation that cedes the real lawmaking authority to administrative agencies. When controversies arise out of regulations adopted by these agencies, members can avoid responsibility by claiming that they did not vote for the objectionable regulations. It becomes impossible, then, for the public to hold their representatives and senators to account. Although the legislation can be promoted as producing some indisputable public good, like clean air or clean water, the voters—and probably the lawmakers themselves—have no way of knowing who is actually going to bear the costs.

Under these circumstances, one can understand why Congress might give up on the difficult task of crafting legislation. If the courts will not carefully review how administrative agencies interpret legislation, there is little point in spending time on it. As described in chapter 2, crafting legislation is an arduous process, and in its best form requires each member of the House and Senate to take a political risk by disappointing or angering some group of constituents. The process produces a focus on specific words, and compromises often come with an agreement on the precise meaning of these words. Under these circumstances, one would assume that the administrative agency with responsibility to enforce the law will be bound by the compromises that Congress struck, but as described in chapter 1, on the rule of law, this does not appear to be true.

It is here that judicial review is important. Unless Congress has acted in violation of the Constitution, those who disagree with a piece of legislation have no basis for challenging it, but they can always challenge the way the agency interprets it. In this case, judicial review under the APA should determine whether the agency has properly interpreted what Congress intended, and a court could determine whether or not the agency went beyond what it was authorized to do by Congress. If the agency properly kept within the scope of what Congress authorized, that should end the challenge. On the other hand, if the agency went beyond what Congress intended, a challenge on that basis would succeed.

A few decisions like this would induce both Congress and administrative agencies to be more careful. Congress would find that the legislative process is worth pursuing and agencies would have to be more careful in what they assert about their statutory authority. However, if *Chevron* is not modified, both these advantages will be lost. The courts will continue to defer to the agencies' interpretations of the statutory language Congress has chosen, and Congress will have fewer incentives to enact legislation that identifies with precision what it wants done. Similarly, the agencies will feel empowered to adopt rules and regulations that Congress might not have had in mind when it enacted the law. It would make sense, then, for Congress to pass laws with broad language for which they can take credit, without worrying excessively about whether they say precisely what they can agree on. Of course, that attitude is then read by the agency as authority to roam even more widely over the territory the law might be interpreted to cover.

Finally, if there were ever any doubt about whether Congress cares about retaining its powers under the Constitution, that doubt is dispelled by its actions in establishing the Consumer Financial Protection Bureau in the 2010 Dodd-Frank Act. Not only did Congress give the CFPB an enormously broad statutory mandate—the agency is to protect consumers from "unfair, deceptive, or abusive acts and practices and from discrimination"—but it actually put the agency outside the control of Congress and the president. First, it established the CFPB as a bureau within the Federal Reserve, an independent agency, and gave it direct funding from the Fed's ample resources. This meant that Congress would not have even its most basic constitutional power over the agency through the appropriations process. Dodd-Frank also provided that the

Fed, which is an independent agency with a bipartisan governing board, would have no control over the CFPB, the Fed's own bureau. And finally Congress put the agency under the control of a single administrator—not a bipartisan board or commission—who would hold office for a term of five years and could not be removed from office by the president except for malfeasance or other dereliction.

These provisions—which in 2016 came under constitutional challenge[17]—hand unfettered authority to a single person engaged in an activity that the Democratic majority in Congress approved, showing that the institutional interests of Congress have become so weakened that Congress will now surrender its most basic functions if doing so can achieve a short-term ideological or political party goal. Unless the judiciary intervenes to enforce discipline, Congress, in its current depleted role in the constitutional system, is a potential danger to the system's survival.

Accordingly, if there is a desire to curb the growth of the administrative state in the future, the courts, and not Congress, will have to do it. That is fully in accord with what the Framers intended, but that means judicial review—now deeply impaired by *Chevron*—will have to be significantly resuscitated.

As Justice Rehnquist said in the benzene case, discussed above:

> [I]f we are ever to reshoulder the burden of ensuring that Congress itself make the critical policy decisions, [cases like this one] are surely the cases in which to do it. It is difficult to imagine a more obvious example of Congress simply avoiding a choice which was both fundamental for purposes of the statute and yet politically so divisive that the necessary decision or compromise was difficult, if not impossible, to hammer out in the legislative forge. Far from detracting from the substantive authority of Congress, a declaration that the first sentence of [the relevant section] of the Occupational Safety and Health Act constitutes an invalid delegation to the Secretary of Labor would preserve the authority of Congress.[18]

In chapter 6, I discuss the current status of the nondelegation doctrine—the idea that under the separation of powers Congress cannot constitutionally delegate what is effectively legislative authority to the president or the agencies of the executive branch. This is a clear imperative for the judiciary under the constitutional structure, but its use has been impeded by the Supreme Court's difficulty in defining legislative authority. Nevertheless, the nondelegation doctrine could be implicated whenever a court determines that an administrative agency has exceeded its statutory authority. That overstepping of the agency's mandate could be simply an overaggressive interpretation by the agency or—as Justice Rehnquist argued in the benzene case—the result of an unconstitutional delegation of legislative authority by Congress.

As we will see in chapters 6 and 7, however, because of the chronic inability of Congress to fully carry out its constitutional responsibilities, a viable nondelegation doctrine may be necessary in reserve before the courts can effectively engage in judicial review of a statute's grant of authority to an agency.

4

Progressivism and the Rise of the Administrative State

Experience should teach us to be most on our guard to protect liberty when the Government's purposes are beneficent. Men born to freedom are naturally alert to repel invasion of their liberty by evil-minded rulers. The greater dangers to liberty lurk in insidious encroachment by men of zeal, well meaning but without understanding.

Justice Louis Brandeis[1]

The roots of the administrative state are deep in the Progressive Era, the period roughly from 1880 to 1920. On the surface, Progressivism was a response to the immense social problems of that time, but it was far more than a simple reform movement. The Progressives developed ideas about government that gave rise to a very different view of the Constitution than had prevailed in the past. These ideas, carried forward by FDR's appointment of seven new Supreme Court justices—all of whom came of age in the Progressive Era—profoundly influenced how the courts have since seen their responsibility in the U.S. constitutional system. In that way, the Progressive ideology had an important role in the growth of the administrative state.

The Underlying Ideas of the Progressive Movement

The fundamental element of Progressivist theory was a belief in the inevitability of change. This, Progressives thought, put their philosophy in conflict with a written constitution. Woodrow Wilson, a leading Progressive thinker, writes of the Constitution's checks and balances:

> The trouble with the theory is that government is not a machine, but a living thing. It falls, not under the theory of the universe, but under the theory of organic life. It is accountable to Darwin, not to Newton. It is modified by its environment, necessitated by its tasks, shaped to its functions by the sheer pressure of life. No living thing can have its organs offset against each other, as checks, and live.[2]

Wilson's references to Newton and Darwin are not metaphoric. Whereas Newton had posited a world that did not change—the earth would revolve around the sun forever—Darwin's theory of evolution, as Progressives saw it, had proven both the certainty of change and the malleability of human nature. These ideas had implications in the political as well as the natural world. Not only could things change, they would *always* change, so the Constitution—framed by men who probably admired Newton and the stable universe he envisioned—would inevitably be an impediment to dealing with the then current problems that the Framers could not have foreseen.

In another representative passage, Wilson writes:

> The makers of the Constitution constructed the federal government upon a theory of checks and balances which was meant to limit the operation of each part and allow to no single part or organ of it a dominating force; but no government can be successfully conducted upon so mechanical a theory. Leadership and control must be lodged somewhere; the whole art of statesmanship is the art of bringing the several parts of government into effective cooperation for the accomplishment of particular common objects.[3]

Nor did Wilson approve of the separation of powers. To him, it is a

> radical defect in our federal system that it parcels out power and confuses responsibility as it does. The main purpose of the Convention of 1787 seems to have been to accomplish this grievous mistake.

The "literary theory" of checks and balances is simply a consistent account of what our constitution-makers tried to do; and those checks and balances have proved mischievous just to the extent to which they have succeeded in establishing themselves as realities.[4]

In his 1887 "Study of Administration," Wilson writes of the "steadily widening...new conceptions of state duty....Administration is everywhere putting its hands to new undertakings. The utility, cheapness, and success of the government's postal service, for instance, point towards the early establishment of governmental control of the telegraph system," he exults. "Seeing every day new things which the state ought to do, the next thing is to see clearly how it ought to do them."[5] A bit later in the article, he continues:

And let me say that large powers and unhampered discretion [for administrators] seem to me the indispensable conditions of responsibility. Public attention must be easily directed, in each case of good or bad administration, to just the man deserving of praise or blame. There is no danger in power, if only it be not irresponsible. If it be divided, dealt out in shares to many, it is obscured; and if it be obscured, it is made irresponsible. But if it be centred in heads of the service and in heads of branches of the service, it is easily watched and brought to book.[6]

In these views, we can see glimmers of the *Chevron* doctrine—the idea that administrators, as disinterested experts, rather than courts, should interpret the scope of their authority.

Here is the crux of the matter. The Framers clearly thought that the judiciary—an independent legal authority—should interpret the laws that Congress passed, but the Progressives believed that expert administrators with unhampered discretion were best equipped for this task. The powerful administrative state with which we are now confronted is the result of the success of this view, together with the Supreme Court's abandonment—during the late New Deal Era and afterward through *Chevron*—of the presumption that it is the judiciary's role to interpret the scope and meaning of the laws that Congress enacts.

These conflicting views foreshadowed the political and legal debates of the present day. Should we stand by the Constitution as the Framers intended it, or ignore it to meet the needs of the time? Do we want the Constitution that the Framers constructed or the "living Constitution" the Progressives envisioned? From the point of view of the Framers, the answer is easy: the purpose of the Constitution is to preserve liberty— that was the lodestar for the authors of the *Federalist Papers*. They might or might not have been influenced by Newton, but they lived in a time when the most serious problem they faced was to devise a government structure that would function effectively (as the Articles of Confederation had not) and still preserve liberty. That is what the Framers hoped their constitutional structure would achieve.

The Progressives, led by Wilson, Theodore Roosevelt, and many others, saw it differently, as do their intellectual descendants today.[7] In their view, as the world and people's attitudes or values evolve, the government's role must also change. What the Progressives saw around them was growing poverty and inequality accompanied by increasingly powerful megacorporations. In this environment, the ideal of liberty had to yield to other goals; the Constitution and the law seemed insufficiently flexible to deal with these challenges. Herbert Hovenkamp explains:

> The separation of law and economics in Progressive legal thought was hastened by Progressives' growing disenchantment with the unregulated market. Progressives doubted the efficacy of markets in a way that no group of American legal thinkers ever had. During their lifetimes they had witnessed technological innovations and a mania for mergers that appeared to transform American industry from one of hundreds of competitive producers to tight oligopolies of a few giant firms.... They had also witnessed the dramatic rise of the family fortunes of the masters of this new wealth, such as the Morgans and the Rockefellers, just as they saw the equally dramatic rise of large scale urban poverty. For the Progressives, the market was at fault on both counts.[8]

Echoing Hovenkamp, Tushnet observes in his 2011 article that "Progressive legal theorists defended the rise of the administrative state. For them, the rapidity of social and economic change rendered the traditional tripartite scheme of government outmoded: neither legislatures nor courts could respond quickly enough, or with enough expertise, to the problems generated by change." Indeed, he writes, "Their examination of the administrative state in operation led them to conclude that administrative agencies ought to be freed from close judicial supervision, at least if the agencies were reformed to fit the Progressives' model."[9]

The Progressives were unnecessarily alarmed; the Framers' Constitution could accommodate change. The constitutional system did not have to be modified in order to accommodate changes in society. From our perspective today, we can see that the Constitution the Progressives so distrusted could easily meet the needs of a country many times the size and infinitely more varied than the country that existed in the Progressive Era. True, not all the problems of this or the Progressive Era have been solved. But consider these large-scale developments: the millions of immigrants who were pouring into the United States during the late 1800s have become productive citizens; the giant corporations whose power the Progressives feared were tamed—not by regulation, but by innovation and the competition it engendered; and, because of rapid changes in the U.S. economy, the rush of people from the farms and rural areas into the cities to work in factories has become a problem of finding enough workers with the skills to operate the automated high-tech production and service facilities now in place. That problem, too, will eventually be solved, and probably by the private sector.

Moreover, because they dismissed the Framers' concern about the preservation of liberty and rejected the idea of an unchanging human nature, Progressives did not see a moral basis for protecting the natural rights of all individuals. This produced one of the darkest periods in American history, with the embrace of eugenics.[10] Today, this element of Progressivism is little known—if it were, those on the left would not now style themselves as progressives rather than as liberals. Their intellectual forebears, however, thought they were following Darwin and "science" when they tried to improve humanity by eliminating undesirables from the gene pool. Few today are aware of the sterilization of over 70,000 people in the United States who were deemed to be genetically defective. For the Progressives, eugenics was "settled science"—a forerunner of the left's views in our own day about climate change. In the 1927 Supreme Court case that approved sterilization, *Buck v. Bell*, the opinion by Chief Justice Oliver Wendell Holmes, joined by Justices Brandeis, Harlan Stone, and five others, contains the infamous line, "Three generations of imbeciles are enough."[11]

Woodrow Wilson, as governor of New Jersey (from 1911 to 1913), signed a forcible sterilization law, which targeted "the hopelessly defective and criminal classes." Wisconsin, the domain of the Progressive hero Robert La Follette, who served as its governor and U.S. senator, passed its forcible sterilization law in 1913, with the slogan "sterilization or racial disaster."[12]

During this period, too, segregation and Jim Crow laws increased broadly throughout the South. Wilson's racist views, which were not unusual at the time, are now well-known.[13] "Even white progressives, North as well as South, did not believe in any sort of equality between the races at the turn of the century," as Michael McGerr writes in his history of the period. "A time of environmentalist thinking, the Progressive Era was equally a time of race thinking. As the nineteenth century ended, science increasingly endorsed many Americans' belief that some races were better than others and that racial characteristics were hereditary and therefore quite possibly unalterable."[14]

Other violations of individual and human rights during the Progressive Era were the "red scare" after World War I; the associated execution, in 1927, of anarchist immigrants Nicola Sacco and Bartolomeo Vanzetti, whose Italian background exacerbated animus against them during their murder trial; the first restrictions on immigration; and Prohibition.[15]

The Progressive Roots of the Administrative State

The Progressives' "extravagant faith in administration," as Thomas C. Leonard writes, was the foundation of their policy ideas. "The visible hand of administrative government, guided by disinterested experts who were university trained and credentialed, would diagnose, treat and even cure low wages, long hours, unemployment, labor conflict, industrial accidents, financial crises, unfair labor practices, deflation, and other ailments of industrial capitalism." Regardless of their different ideas about one problem or another, "nearly all ultimately agreed that the best means to their several ends was the administrative state."[16]

The Progressives' faith in administration also implied major changes in government structure. The government that came out of the Civil War was still largely in the form that the Framers had devised. Congress was the dominant player, as the Framers expected it to be, and the courts—despite the need for some departures under the exigencies of the war—still kept the growth of the executive branch well under control. Post–Civil War presidents made few efforts to expand their political or policy territory, but intellectual currents for change were beginning to stir. One of the most influential of these was Wilson's study of the power of Congress, *Congressional Government*, published in 1885, which anticipated and endorsed the coming struggle by the Progressives to increase the power of administration—in other words, the executive branch—in relation to Congress.

Wilson, who favored a strong executive, complained about the "blind worship" of the Constitution's principles, and was later to write that the Constitution should be substantially changed. He noted with disapproval the fact that the courts had failed to check the growing power of Congress after the Civil War, and, as noted above, he regarded the legislature—not the executive—as "the aggressive spirit." In his view, "the subtle, stealthy, almost imperceptible encroachments of policy, of political action" are "the precedents upon which additional prerogatives are generally reared; and yet these are the very encroachments with which it is hardest for the courts to deal, and concerning which, accordingly, the federal courts have declared themselves unauthorized to hold any opinions."[17] Ironically, the latter-day intellectual descendants of Wilson and other Progressives, as we will see, would now argue that the courts should *not* interfere with the work of administrative agencies or challenge the new balance of power in which the executive branch is the dominant player.

Wilson was an advocate for the growth of the administrative state before anyone understood the term. In his highly influential "Study of Administration," he saw a role for it that is far different from anything that might have been contemplated by the Framers. While today we might see the power of the administrative state as ultimately authorized and limited by legislation, Wilson's view was that "administration in the United States must be at all points sensitive to public opinion."[18] This implies a completely different concept of government from that contemplated by the Constitution. For Wilson, administrative agencies were not simply acting on the instructions of Congress or even the president; they were to be the government itself in the sense that they were to understand in some way what the public wanted and carry it out. How this was to happen is not clear from Wilson's writings, which sometimes seem deliberately obscure. He seemed to believe that the American people were moving toward a common will of some kind, that a legislature was not essential to resolve conflicting interests, and that expert administrators—perhaps with general guidance from Congress—would themselves be able to recognize and implement what the people as a whole wanted to happen.

If this notion of administrators sensitive to public opinion seems Hegelian, it is. There is much in Wilson's thinking that is quite alien to the idea of democracy as expressed through a legislature. He and many other Progressives, following Hegel and Rousseau, thought of the people's *will* as the key determinant of government policy, though they never defined how that will would be discerned. "Wilson conceded," writes Ronald Pestritto, a scholar of Wilson's thought, "that his conception of modern democracy—where leaders must discern the implicit will of society—did not comport with the traditional understanding of democratic government." As Wilson saw it, according to Pestritto, "this governance by educated experts is democratic in a much higher sense: the experts in the civil service will not be distracted by the contending of special interests in majoritarian politics, but will instead discern the true and implicit unified will of the nation."[19]

Indeed, during the Progressive Era, the federal government's role in the economy substantially increased, primarily through the establishment of new administrative agencies. The Interstate Commerce Act, which created the Interstate Commerce Commission (ICC) to regulate the railroads, was passed in 1887, and the ICC was later strengthened with the Hepburn Act in 1906 and the Mann-Elkins Act in 1910. The Food and Drug Act was passed in 1906; the Sixteenth Amendment (income tax), the Seventeenth Amendment (direct election of senators), and the Federal Reserve Act all became law in 1913; and likewise the Federal Trade Commission Act and the Clayton Antitrust Act in 1914.

The rights of individuals, so important to the Framers, were of little account to Wilson, who said in his book, *The State*:

> No student of history can wisely censure those who protest against state paternalism. It by no means follows, nevertheless, that because the state may unwisely interfere in the life of the individual, it must be pronounced in itself and by nature a necessary evil. It is no more an evil than is society itself. It is the organic body of society: without it society would be hardly more than a mere abstraction.[20]

Thus the roots of Progressivism are deep in statism—emphasizing the importance of the state or the government relative to the individual. It is not hard to see that this ideology would emphasize how to free government power and government growth from the restrictions of the Framers' constitutional system. This is the view that came back to prominence and power in the New Deal and laid a foundation in legal theory that still seems to guide the judiciary today.

Progressivism and the New Deal

In an essay in a 2016 edited volume on Progressivism, Ken Kersch argues that any connection between contemporary liberalism and Progressivism is a conservative concoction. "Conservatives never explain," he writes, "that modern American liberalism and the postwar Left were forged both as an outgrowth of, and in reaction against, Progressivism."[21] Modern conservatives certainly accept that modern liberals do not hold the views of Progressives on sterilization, racism, or the other inexcusable features of the Progressive Era. Nevertheless, it is difficult for liberals and the Left to disclaim any connection with Progressivism when they, too, support a "living Constitution" and a powerful administrative state—both affronts to the constitutional structure that were born in the Progressive Era.

This is not to say that philosophical or political links cannot be found between modern liberals' view of the administrative state and the Progressive view that government is best run by a credentialed class that can better discern the will of the people than can a legislature. The Progressives, like liberals today, were members of that educated and credentialed class; a powerful administrative state would have given this class more power at a time when business and finance were becoming increasingly dominant in the United States. In his important work, *Is Administrative Law Unlawful?*, Philip Hamburger points out that during the Progressive Era administrative law could have been "an instrument of a class that took a dim view of popularly elected legislatures and a high view of its own rationality and specialized knowledge.... Although it did not thereby become the only ruling class, it at least made itself the *rulemaking* class."[22]

Woodrow Wilson was elected president in 1912, and served two terms. Thomas Leonard notes:

> If an administrative state were to be the new guarantor of economic progress, it would need to be built. By March 1917, the end of Woodrow Wilson's first term, it was. Countless additions would later be made to the new regulatory edifice, but the "fourth branch" of government was established.... The US government now directly taxed personal incomes, corporations, and estates. It dissolved prominent industrial combinations in steel, oil, tobacco, and sugar. Its new Federal Reserve regulated money, credit, and banking. Its new Federal Trade Commission supervised domestic industry.... State and federal labor legislation mandated workmen's compensation, banned child labor, compelled schooling of children, inspected factories, fixed minimum wages and maximum hours...and much more."[23]

The administrative state was on its way. In a sense, however, Progressivism had gained strong support among the American people well before Wilson won the presidency. As Hovenkamp has observed, "In 1905, Justice Holmes complained in his *Lochner v. New York* dissent that the revolution had already occurred: the majority's decision striking down a ten-hour law for bakers 'is decided upon an economic theory which a large part of the country does not entertain.'"[24]

Yet the Progressives' victory was not permanent. It was "impossible," as Richard Hofstadter, writing in 1955, notes, "that a mood so completely dominant in, say, 1912 should have evaporated without any trace ten years later. Yet what stands out [in the 1920s] is the extent to which Progressivism had either disappeared or transmuted its form...." In 1912 "Progressive sentiment had been so general in the country that Taft, the only avowed conservative in the field, could not, even with the aid of several state machines and ample funds, muster so much as one fourth of the total vote."[25] Nevertheless, after Wilson's two terms, in the elections of 1920, 1924, and 1928 the country chose three Republican presidents, who (with the possible exception of Hoover) had more traditional views of the Constitution. The Court followed the election returns during this period. Felix Frankfurter, a Progressive, who later became a justice of the Supreme Court, wrote (in a 1930 lecture series) that since 1920 the Court had "invalidated more [Progressive] legislation than in the fifty years preceding" and "always by a divided Court, always over the protest of its most distinguished minds!"[26]

No one can know what would have happened in the United States if the Great Depression had not occurred, Roosevelt had not been elected in 1932, and the New Deal had not turned into a full-bore restoration of Progressive political ideas.[27] Given the exigencies of the Depression, it should not be surprising that the Progressive idea of creating administrative agencies to address societal problems returned once again as a governing philosophy. But it was the legal theories developed by the justices whom FDR appointed during his second and third terms that gave the administrative state its staying power. Even today—well after the emergency environment of the Depression Era—the idea that administrative agencies should be given latitude to operate, or are better equipped than courts to interpret congressional statutes, continues to support the growth and power of the administrative state.

Each of Roosevelt's appointees was born between 1882 (Frankfurter and James F. Byrnes) and 1898 (William O. Douglas). That means that the youngest were adults by the end of the Wilson administration, and were thus fully imbued with the ethos of the Progressive Era during their formative period. When they got to the Supreme Court, they were not strangers to the idea that the traditional ways the Constitution had been interpreted had to be modified in order to justify major new responsibilities for the government.[28] That, as much as anything else, was responsible for the growth of the administrative state during and after the New Deal, as shown in figure 4.1.

FIGURE 4.1

The Growth of the Federal Workforce in the New Deal Period

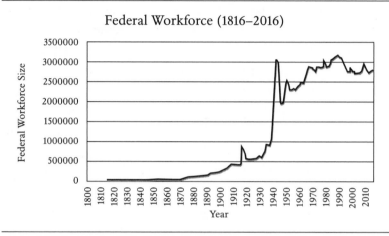

Source: U.S. Bureau of Labor Statistics; Federal Reserve Bank of St. Louis; and Historical Statistics of the United States. Compiled by Ryan Nabil of the American Enterprise Institute.

Progressive Views Revived in the New Deal

Progressive thought was a key element in the growth of the New Deal. Many of the members of the Roosevelt administration saw the New Deal as a restoration of the underlying ideas of Progressivism, which had been submerged during the Republican administrations of the 1920s. As described by Hovenkamp, the foundations of Progressive thought—"its distrust of the market, and its faith that the government agency, whose salaried officials did not profit from their decisions, could regulate the economy better"—had a long-lasting effect on American governance. This occurred, he writes, in two stages: "first during the Progressive Era and later during the New Deal, progressive policy makers erected the modern administrative state which removed great parts of the economy from free market control and subordinated concerns for the efficient use of resources to other values that were much more difficult to articulate."[29]

New Deal legislation between 1933 and 1938 "made the enactments of the Progressive Era seem timid by comparison," Hofstadter notes. These legislative changes "in their totality carried the politics and administration of the United States farther from conditions of 1914 than those had been from the conditions of 1880."[30] Hofstadter in fact claims that the New Deal was different from anything that had yet happened in the United States: "different because its central problem was unlike the problems of Progressivism; different in its ideas and its spirit and its techniques."[31]

This is doubtful. Looked at from the perspective of 2018 and the growth of the administrative state, the New Deal was just like the Progressive Era, only bigger. The Franklin Roosevelt presidency seems simply to have expanded on what Wilson—the consummate Progressive—sought to do during his presidency: deal with economic concerns through regulation and increase the size and reach of government in the economy. What the New Deal created is still with us, and the Progressive ideas that started the process—principally the notion that the government is a cure for what ails the economy—is the foundation of the administrative state. As John Maynard Keynes said in 1936, "the ideas of economists and political philosophers, both when they are right and when they are wrong, are more powerful than is commonly understood. Indeed the world is ruled by little else."[32]

A number of academics argue that the New Deal was not an ideological period like the Progressive Era but simply a pragmatic response to the severe economic problems of the day. For example, Kersch notes that, "although attacked [by conservatives] for abandoning constitutional rules and restraints for ever-shifting policy imperatives, the New Deal was famously pragmatic and untheorized."[33] This is mythmaking. Rexford Guy Tugwell, one of the most influential members of FDR's Brain Trust, in a 1927 remark lamented the fact that World War I had ended *too early*: "We were on the verge of having an international industrial machine when peace broke. Only the Armistice prevented a great experiment in control of production, control of prices, and control of consumption."[34] Unless Tugwell had radically changed his views by the time he became a powerful figure in the Roosevelt administration, "pragmatic and untheorized" would not be an apt description of his contribution to New Deal policies.

Indeed, the Progressives' faith in administrative agencies was anything but pragmatic, considering what we know now about how a complex economy actually works. For example, James M. Landis, one of the strongest proponents of Progressive views in administrative law, wrote in his well-known 1938 book, *The Administrative Process*, about the importance of "control over the economic forces which affect the life of the community":

> [E]xpertness [in an administrator]...springs only from that continuity of interest, that ability and desire to devote fifty-two weeks a year, year after year, to a particular problem.... [T]he art of regulating an industry requires knowledge of the details of its operation, ability to shift requirements as the condition of the industry may dictate, the pursuit of energetic measures upon the appearance of an emergency, and the power through enforcement to realize conclusions as to policy.[35]

In other words, even as late as 1938, the Progressives believed that government agencies would actually be controlling—perhaps even directly operating—the businesses in a regulated industry. It's no wonder that when Progressive legal thought was finally triumphant at the end of the New Deal, it favored giving ultimate control to administrative agencies engaged in regulation, with relatively little interference from the courts.

However, even as administrative agencies were beginning to operate throughout the economy, Progressive enthusiasts were disappointed when they watched these organizations in action. From the perspective of the early twenty-first century, it should come as no surprise that administrative agencies were a disappointment to the Progressives who had expected so much from them. How were the Progressive theorists to know—contrary to their idealized assumptions—that administrators were not equal to the task of regulating complex competitive industries, were no more "expert" than the courts at understanding what Congress had authorized, were likely to be well educated but plodding and unimaginative, were no match for the industry experts and lawyers deployed against them, and would treat the industries they regulated as protectees when challenged by nonindustry competitors—a phenomenon so pervasive as to have a name: clientelism.

Problems began to show up as early as 1924. A study by Gerard Henderson, one of Frankfurter's students, concluded that "in the long run, and until current ideals of public service change very radically, it cannot be expected that a government commission, paying modest salaries and exposed to the vicissitudes of political life, can command the services of those supermen whose decisions are always made of the substance of justice and wisdom."[36] By 1930, Frankfurter's own complaints were becoming more urgent: looking at the work of the Federal Power Commission, Frankfurter noted that "a few subordinates, subjected to great temptations and with appropriations from Congress so meager as to starve their efforts, [were] hardly equipped to meet complacency and legalism within the Commission and the pressure of acute and powerful forces without."[37]

Lawyer and economist I. Leo Sharfman wrote five volumes on the ICC, which Frankfurter called "a monumental work." The first volume, published in 1931, "reflected the Progressive vision in almost pristine form," as Tushnet notes. But "by 1937, when the final volume appeared, Sharfman's perspective had shifted subtly as New Deal experience accumulated."[38] Tushnet further explains:

> Sharfman published his final volumes after the nation had seen how some New Deal agencies operated, and the later books had a slightly more skeptical and less enthusiastic tone than the first volumes.... Responding in part to political challenges to the New Deal's administrative apparatus and in part to their new understanding of how agencies actually operated, the Progressives' heirs began to offer a more chastened view of the modern administrative state.[39]

What happened next was fully to be expected. It turned out that the administrators—even if "experts"—did not know enough to control whole industries. In fact, they needed a lot of education by the industries they were supposed to control.

Although this alarmed Progressives, who saw administrative agencies as adversaries of the private sector, agencies became more like collaborators than regulators. As government grew, crony capitalism found fertile ground. What regulatory agencies were really good for was negotiating with industries about the decisions they intended to make and the rules and regulations they intended to issue. Congress tried to level the playing field with the adoption of the Administrative Procedure Act in 1946, which encouraged rulemaking through an administrative proposal followed by a comment period, with the agency ultimately describing why it made the decisions it did. Industries and firms would have their innings with the agency, and if still aggrieved would have resort to the courts, which the APA endorsed by calling judicial review "essential." But courts cannot do anything about crony capitalism, even if they can spot it.

"Toward the end of the 1930s," Tushnet writes, "Progressive theorists found themselves pressed to defend the democratic legitimacy of administrative agencies...but the more perceptive of them began to develop the idea that agency processes themselves could be a form of democratic participation in decisionmaking." Quoting the legal scholar Walter Gellhorn, Tushnet says that the latter "argued in 1941 that the very procedures designed to ensure fairness to the subjects of regulation also 'democratize[d] our government processes,' because they '[brought] to the interests and individuals immediately affected an opportunity to shape the course of regulation, modeling it to fit the contours of their own special problems.'" Tushnet further quotes Gellhorn as saying, "'A real picture of government regulation of an industry would not always show two scowling antagonists, but rather more often two smiling collaborators.'"[40] This image would have had the original Progressive advocates for administrative power turning in their graves.

Thus the powerful agencies envisioned by the Progressives—forcing whole industries to bend to the "public interest" through their disinterested expertise—were to be transmuted into places where rules, regulations, and adjudicative decisions would be negotiated out, with administrators theoretically representing the public interest.

But the Progressive view of how the "public interest" can be determined was wrong. In a democracy, only Congress can speak for the public. There is no sense in which a government agency can fully represent the interests of the public at large. Administrative agencies have no more right to speak for the public interest than do the courts. Nevertheless, this idea that an agency can resolve conflicting interests is the essential Progressive vision that underlies *Chevron*.

Progressive Theories on Administrative Law
Accepted by the Supreme Court

Progressive legal thought was certainly triumphant in the New Deal, especially after 1937, when FDR was able to appoint almost a completely new Supreme Court, but this book is focused primarily on only one important element of the Supreme Court's administrative law decisions—the deference that the courts must accord to administrative agency interpretations of their statutory authorities. These are the decisions that gave significant impetus to the administrative state and enabled it to grow to its current position of dominance within the U.S. government.

For the Supreme Court, the principal issue during much of the New Deal was the nature of administrative decision making and the degree to which it had to meet the standards of a trial in order to produce a result acceptable to a court. Sometimes this controversy is presented as a case of two different systems in collision—lawyers and judges trusting only heavily judicialized proceedings and administrators hoping to resolve issues expeditiously.[41] As Tushnet notes, "the Progressive agenda for administrative law was, in essence, to liberate agencies from judicial supervision so that technocracy guided loosely by politics could replace law. Nothing the Court could do other than withdraw completely from the field would have comported with that agenda."[42] This is the correct formulation of the issue. The Progressives' purpose was to liberate administrative agencies from judicial supervision, and as we will see, that is what happened. *Chevron*, the 1984 decision of a unanimous Supreme Court, as discussed in detail in chapter 7, is the apotheosis of this Progressive effort.

Speaking of the question in terms of liberating administrative agencies from the judiciary obscures the fact that there were serious constitutional issues involved, as shown by a 1936 rate-making case, in which the secretary of agriculture attempted to fix the rates for the services of the St. Joseph Stock Yards Company. The secretary had the authority from Congress to set these rates, but for the Court (Chief Justice Hughes) the question was whether the secretary's rates were confiscatory and thus a violation of the Fifth Amendment:

[T]he Constitution fixes limits to the ratemaking power by prohibiting the deprivation of property without due process of law.... When the Legislature acts directly, its action is subject to judicial scrutiny and determination in order to prevent the transgression of these limits of power. The Legislature cannot preclude that scrutiny or determination by any declaration or legislative finding. Legislative declaration or finding is necessarily subject to independent judicial review upon the facts and the law by courts of competent jurisdiction to the end that the Constitution, as the supreme law of the land, may be maintained.[43]

So the Court was not simply an officious intermeddler here—wedded to outmoded ideas about the superiority of courts over administrative decision making—but saw itself as fulfilling its role as the defender of the Constitution. In this case, as it happens, the Court held that no confiscation was shown. But in a subsequent case, *Morgan v. United States*, argued and decided in the same year, the Court struck down a similar rate-making decision by the secretary of agriculture because the proceedings within the Agriculture Department did not afford the appellant the "full hearing" the statute required. Both cases can be seen as judicial efforts to control the administrative process.

But 1937 was a turning point. FDR's court-packing plan failed, but the Supreme Court never thereafter declared—as it had in the *Schechter* and *Panama Refining* cases, discussed in chapter 6—that Congress had unconstitutionally delegated legislative power to the president or to an administrative agency. More important, however, was the fact that justices began to retire—one in 1937 (replaced by Hugo Black), another in 1938 (replaced by Stanley Reed), two in 1939 (replaced by Felix Frankfurter and William Douglas), one in 1940 (replaced by Francis Murphy), two in 1941 (replaced by James Byrnes and Robert Jackson), and one in 1943 (replaced by Wiley Rutledge). Most significant, Harlan Fisk Stone succeeded Charles Evans Hughes as chief justice in 1941. Thus by 1943 FDR had appointed all nine justices and—given the Roosevelt administration's desire for a more compliant Court—all were likely to be supporters of Progressive ideas about administration and administrative law. As Tushnet points out about these justices, "the Progressive critique of traditional doctrines of administrative law gave them clear ideas about how to move forward."[44]

These ideas were generous toward administrative agencies, even though weaknesses in the administrative process were being noted in academic studies by Henderson, Sharfman, and Gellhorn. In a 1941 case, *Gray v. Powell*, for example, the question was whether a railroad that had the right to mine coal on certain land was a "producer" of the coal it mined, and thus entitled to an exemption from a tax on the coal's sale. The firm, a railroad, had hired a contractor to do the mining and deliver the coal for the railroad's use. Congress had not included in the relevant act any definition of exempt coal, so the decision was left to the Department of the Interior as the administrator of the act. The agency concluded that the railroad was not the "producer" of the coal, and the case reached the Supreme Court.

Justice Reed, writing for the Court, concluded in words that echoed the Progressive catechism:

> Congress, which could have legislated specifically as to the individual exemptions [from the tax], found it more efficient to delegate that function to those whose experience in a particular field gave promise of a better informed, more equitable, adjustment of the conflicting interests of price stabilization, upon the one hand, and producer consumption, upon the other.... Where, as here, a determination has been left to an administrative body, this delegation will be respected, and the administrative conclusion left untouched.[45]

Anyone can see a precursor of *Chevron* in these words. There is no reason to believe—as there was none in *Chevron*—that Congress had deliberately left the decision to the agency. An alternative construction might be that Congress saw no need to define the term "producer" because it recognized that the use of coal by the owner of the coal did not implicate the purpose of the act, which was to enable an agency to stabilize the price of coal. Indeed, a dissent by Justice Owen Roberts, in which Chief Justice Stone and Justice Byrnes joined, argued, "There are limits to which administrative officers and courts may appropriately go in reconstructing a statute so as to accomplish aims which the legislature might have had, but which the statute itself, and its legislative history, do not disclose. The present decision, it seems to me, passes that limitation."[46]

Justice Roberts then proceeded with an analysis of the kind that courts would normally do when interpreting a statute, showing that the purpose of the statute—to enable the agency to stabilize the price of coal in interstate commerce—is not served by the majority's reading, since the coal never reaches the market when it is mined by an independent contractor and delivered to the coal's owner.

These two cases, *St. Joseph Stock Yards* and *Gray v. Powell*, bracket a critical period in which the Progressive view of administrative agencies was cemented into Supreme Court precedents. In 1936 the Court emphasized the importance of judicial review to preserve constitutional rights and control the administrative agency, while in 1941 the Court backed away from judicial review in favor of giving freer rein to the decision of an administrative agency. This was a triumph of the Progressive view that has led to a more powerful and intrusive administrative state.

Richard Epstein summarizes it well:

> The classical liberal conception of the Constitution had a long historical run of about 150 years, but in the end it was vanquished by the progressive counterrevolution that culminated in critical Supreme Court decisions, on issues of both federalism and individual rights, during the tumultuous 1930s. It should not be supposed, however, that the progressive mindset in constitutional law has vanished from the current intellectual scene simply because many New Deal Depression-era short-term public works and relief programs no longer form a part of the modern American political fabric.[47]

Indeed, that Progressive mindset is still with us, but now comes in a more benign form. It appears to have no ideology, only a concern that a conservative revival of the classical liberal conception of the Constitution will take away all the good things the government has given us since the New Deal.

In an opinion piece for the *New York Times* in 2017, Emily Bazelon and Eric Posner expressed this pragmatic approach: "Congress is a cumbersome body that moves slowly in the best of times, while the economy is an incredibly dynamic system. For the sake of business as well as labor, the updating of regulations can't wait for Congress to give highly specific and detailed directions." This is followed by a panegyric to the administrative state:

> The New Deal filled the gap [left by a slow-moving Congress] by giving policy-making authorities to agencies, including the Securities and Exchange Commission, which protects investors, and the National Labor Relations Board, which oversees collective bargaining between unions and employers. Later came other agencies, including the Environmental Protection Agency, the Occupational Safety and Health Administration (which regulates workplace safety) and the Department of Homeland Security. Still other agencies regulate the broadcast spectrum, keep the national parks open, help farmers and assist Americans who are overseas."[48]

There appears to be no thought here about what the public might actually want, or—if the slow-moving Congress is now to be displaced—where these agencies get their authority to "make policy." Woodrow Wilson solved this problem, ostensibly, by saying that administrators would (somehow) discern the public's *will*. If asked, Bazelon and Posner would probably not say that; after the twentieth-century experience of fascism and communism, Wilson's authoritarian attitude is now out of style. But there remains a fundamental question that can't simply be ignored, certainly in the face of Brexit: Where does this all-powerful administrative state acquire its moral authority, its legitimacy, to make rules the rest of society must obey? This was the problem with Progressivism in the Progressive Era, and it is still a problem for the (lowercase) progressives today.

If the growth of the administrative state continues, with an increasing number of rules issued by agencies with diminishing moral authority, the American people will eventually recognize that they are no longer in control of their own government. Then, similar to the challenge the EU faces with Brexit, the U.S. government will confront its own crisis of legitimacy.

5

WAS THE PROGRESSIVE FAITH IN ECONOMIC REGULATION JUSTIFIED?

What gives to the individuals as much freedom as is compatible with
life in society is the operation of the market economy. The constitutions
and bills of rights do not create freedom. They merely protect the freedom
that the competitive economic system grants to the individuals against
encroachments on the part of the police power.

LUDWIG VON MISES, *THE ANTI-CAPITALISTIC MENTALITY*[1]

The Progressives' distrust of markets, and faith in government administration and regulation, begun in the Wilson administration and expanded in the New Deal, laid the groundwork for the administrative state. Although the deficiencies of government economic regulation began to come to light even as the New Deal structure was being put in place, the growth of the administrative state has not significantly decelerated since the 1930s. Today, very few observers—even regulation's supporters—would argue that it is an unalloyed good. It is simply a necessity, they believe, to avoid the problems they expect from an unregulated market. This is a weak foundation for something so pervasive and costly as the administrative state, and it is time for some serious questions about whether regulation in general is entitled to the important role it plays in today's U.S. economy.

Why is it necessary for the government to issue over three thousand regulations each year? The number of new laws is relatively few, but the number of new regulations based on laws that Congress passed many years ago never seems to diminish. This is somewhat counterintuitive. One would think that after a new law is enacted there would be a flurry of regulations defining its terms and filling in the details, but after that no large number of additional regulations would be necessary. Yet the Labor Department is still putting out rules under the Fair Labor Standards Act of 1938, the EPA is still issuing regulations under the Clean Air Act of 1970, and the Education Department's controversial bathroom rule was issued under Title IX of the Education Amendments of 1972. Whatever one thinks of the particular rules issued under these laws, it seems implausible that thousands of new ones each year are necessary to keep the American people from harm.

This is a book about how to control the growth of the administrative state, not how to limit regulation per se. But given the fact that rules and regulations are the principal output of the administrative state it seems reasonable to consider what will happen if, as this book proposes, the courts actually restrain this activity. The number of regulations will almost certainly decline as courts look more closely at what Congress specifically authorized. That might or might not be a good thing, depending on one's view of unregulated markets, but this chapter argues that the deficiencies associated with economic regulation support a much tighter rein on the administrative state. Indeed, later in this chapter, we will see that in the few cases in which major regulations have been repealed, the ensuing competition improved services to consumers and lowered their cost. This suggests, at least, that if the courts begin to do what the Framers expected them to do, the results for the American people will be more than satisfactory.

We have become so inured to economic regulation that we don't imagine there are alternatives, but the fact is that markets can function well—often better—without government regulation. Among Adam Smith's many insights in *The Wealth of Nations* is his observation that "it is not from the benevolence of the butcher, the brewer, or the baker, that we expect our dinner, but from their regard for their own interests."[2] Underlying this crisp summary of how an "invisible hand" guides a free-market economy is another seemingly obvious but profound idea— that in a private transaction between two parties both are acting voluntarily and both are getting what they want; otherwise, the transaction would not occur at all.

Finally, there is the enormous power of competition. When I was in college (in the 1960s), one of my professors argued that it was necessary to have a big and powerful government in order to control big and powerful companies like General Motors (there are always arguments like this to justify big government). GM, of course, was eventually "controlled"—to the point that the government had to rescue it from bankruptcy—but not tamed by the government; it was tamed by Toyota, a company that built a better car at lower cost.

In light of the seriousness of these ideas—self-interested activity by individuals drives productive activity; private agreements, consistent with personal liberty, serve the interests of both parties to a transaction; and competition drives innovation and price improvement—some might wonder why there is so much economic regulation in the United States. One reason is that many Americans, especially those with left-of-center political views, do not accept the premises outlined above; many generations later, they remain in thrall to the Progressive ideas of the late nineteenth and early twentieth centuries. To them, transactions of the kind described above create winners and losers, whether or not the losers realize it, and in this view who is the winner and who the loser is determined by unfair power relationships. Similarly, they do not see competition as improving quality, stimulating innovation, or lowering prices; to many Progressives, a market not subject to political intervention provides a foundation for unfair exploitation of the weak by the strong. Oddly, the government, the most powerful, monopolistic, and heavy-handed player of all, is seen as the most benign, and the most likely to act fairly, when in fact it is the easiest tool for powerful interests to bend in their favor. As the Progressives found to their disappointment, crony capitalism grows alongside the growth of government.

By simply looking at what is happening around them, present-day Progressives should recognize that most of the U.S. economy functions quite well without significant economic regulation, and that the regulated part often functions very poorly in comparison with the parts that are not regulated. Let's compare, for example, the housing finance industry and the housing construction industry. The former is controlled by the

FIGURE 5.1
Regulation and Housing Supply

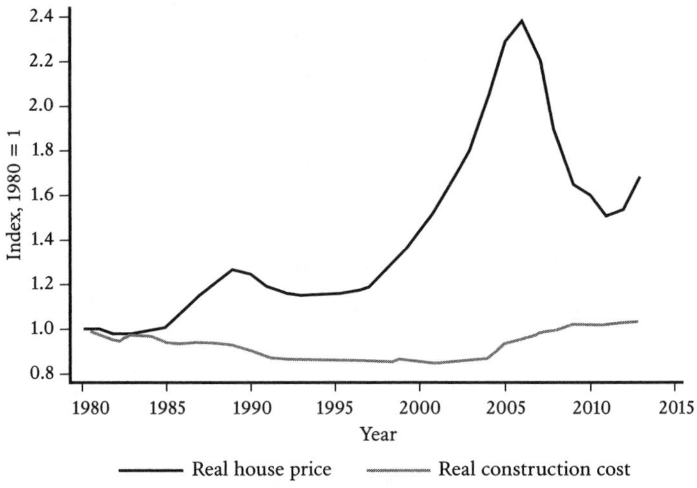

Source: Joseph Gyourko and Raven Malloy, "Regulation and Housing Supply," NBER Working Paper No. 20536 (October 2014), 2. http://www.nber.org/papers/w20536.

government; the latter is a private market in which real estate developers and individuals negotiate prices with contractors. It's not hard to tell from figure 5.1 which is functioning better. The housing finance market is highly unstable, with huge booms and destructive busts; the housing construction market is stable over time.

This is not an artifact of the housing industry. Figure 5.2 shows that the automobile market, in which consumers negotiate with sellers, is also stable in terms of real household median income, despite the fact that auto quality has been increasing over time. Obviously, what is happening is that auto manufacturers, under the pressures of competition, have had to keep improving their product while maintaining or reducing their costs.

We also take for granted the power of competition to reduce the costs of what we buy from "the butcher, the brewer, or the baker" for our dinner. Where I live, the local Safeway offers a fully roasted chicken for $4.95, roughly half the national minimum wage *per hour*. In other words, one can feed a family of three or four with one hour of work at

FIGURE 5.2

Average Real New Car Price/Real Household Median Income (With 1967 = 1)

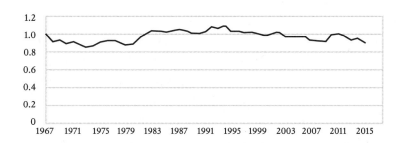

Source: Compiled by Jacob Ward, Vehicle Technologies Program, U.S. Department of Energy, from the following sources: Robert J. Gordon, *The Measurement of Durable Goods Prices*, National Bureau of Economic Research Monograph (Chicago: University of Chicago Press, 1990); and U.S. Department of Commerce, Bureau of Economic Analysis, National Income and Product Accounts (2015), https://www.bea.gov/national/.

the minimum wage. That a chicken can be raised to full size, slaughtered, packaged, shipped, kept fresh, and ultimately roasted and delivered to store shelves for as little as $4.95 is a remarkable fact, and must be credited to the efficiencies and innovations that a competitive market system produces.

The relevance of all this to the growth of the administrative state is clear. Although large sectors of the economy could and do function well without substantial regulation, the economy is saddled with a huge number of unnecessary regulatory and administrative restraints as a legacy of the Progressive movement and the New Deal. An in-depth *New York Times* article in late 2017 recounted the regulatory burden on an apple grower in upstate New York. With their typical thoroughness the *Times* reporters examined all regulations applicable to the orchard and excluded those that were applicable generally to all businesses, identifying "at least 17 federal regulations with about 5,000 restrictions and rules that were relevant to orchards."[3] Apples—and probably roasted chickens—would be even less expensive without the multitude of rules that their producers must follow.

Why So Many Regulations?

The very existence of administrative agencies offers a ready-made solution to Congress when a problem is identified. First, agencies are often able to find within their authorizing legislation the necessary authority to address a problem that some group says deserves attention, even though the issue was not recognized by Congress when it enacted the underlying law. Where that authority does not already exist, the agencies are only too happy to assist Congress in drafting the necessary remedial laws, which are often drafted broadly enough to enable the agency to expand its jurisdiction in the future. For example, the Federal Reserve was a major source of the language in Dodd-Frank that gave broad new powers to...the Federal Reserve. Even when Congress deliberately seeks to restrict what an agency can do, the agency can slip its bonds; witness the CFPB's effort, discussed in chapter 1, to control auto financing when Congress had explicitly excluded that from the agency's jurisdiction. The grant of broad powers to administrative agencies is why apple growers now have to comply with five thousand rules.

While Congress may be partly to blame for failing to restrain itself, the continued and unrestrained growth of the administrative state seems to depend primarily on the willingness of the judiciary to accept administrative agencies' interpretations of their own authority. The Supreme Court's 1984 *Chevron* decision, discussed in detail in chapter 7, is the clearest and most important example of this approach; it even holds that where Congress has been silent on a point, it should be *presumed* that Congress intended to grant the agency the necessary authority to resolve it, and that an administrative agency's interpretation of its own authority is entitled to deference if it is "reasonable." As explained elsewhere, this substantially restricts the judiciary's role in the checks and balances system devised by the Framers, and has resulted in a runaway regulatory state.

Occasionally, as also discussed elsewhere, the courts' retreat from reviewing administrative rulemaking is lauded as "judicial restraint"—often by conservatives. This is certainly justified when the issue is a matter of policy, which belongs to the elected branches; but when the issue is whether the agency is exceeding its statutory authority there is little doubt the Framers intended that the judiciary would decide this question, and that continued judicial exercise of this power is a necessary element of checks and balances, the separation of powers, and the rule of law.

Recognition of this point would not be a resuscitation of what was called "substantive due process"—where certain laws were overturned because of the Supreme Court's view that Congress did not have the constitutional authority to enact them—but simply a return to what the Constitution says about the authority of the judiciary: "The judicial Power shall extend to all cases, in Law and Equity, arising under this Constitution, the Laws of the United States, and Treaties made, or which shall be made, under their Authority" (Article III, Section 2). As has been noted, in *Marbury* Chief Justice Marshall interpreted this language to mean that "[i]t is emphatically the province and duty of the judicial department to say what the law is." And the same idea is also included in the Administrative Procedure Act, which makes clear that the courts should have the power of "judicial review" over administrative rules and regulations. It is difficult to see how we could have the rule of law—and a system in which the laws are actually made by the representatives of the people—unless we have some kind of judicial control over the authority of administrative agencies to interpret the scope of the power they were given.

The balance of this chapter tries to make clear that regulations—which are clearly necessary in some cases—do not represent the public interest merely because they emanate from government agencies. As the examples in this chapter show, economic and financial regulations are as likely to be harmful to the economy as they are to be helpful. Moreover, they are as likely to be based on the agency's need to impress Congress, justify an increase in its appropriations, and extend the agency's power, or on effective lobbying of the agency by a powerful interest group, as on any other grounds. Congress certainly has the power to authorize agency rulemaking, but that authority has to be limited by the scope of what Congress actually intended when the underlying law was passed, and it should be up to the judiciary—not the administrative agency—to decide this question.

Even assuming that much of the regulation enacted in the Progressive Era and the New Deal was necessary at the time, it may be unnecessary today. One of the fears of the Progressive movement, for example, described more fully in chapter 4, was that the very large companies that were developing in the late-nineteenth-century economy would become so powerful as to take control of the political system and the government. We now know that if competition and innovation are allowed to do their work, this does not happen. My AEI colleague Mark Perry has noted that the 2017 *Fortune 500* list of companies includes only sixty companies that appeared on the 1955 list (less than 12 percent).[4] This is the effect of creative destruction—the constant economic renewal that comes about through competition. Consumers—that is, the public—weed out those firms that are not providing relative value. Indeed, the only cases where companies attain near immunity from the creative destruction of competition is where they are protected by regulation.

The most likely explanation for why we have so many regulations is that we have so many administrative agencies; these agencies, in turn, believe that making new rules is necessary to show Congress how important they are. As discussed in the chapter on Congress, there is often a constituency that supports these rules, and for congressional oversight committees it is not worth their time to fight about whether any agency should have issued a particular rule. The worst consequence for the agency is a tongue lashing from a senator. Thus, in what is an extreme form of what economists call "path dependency"—mindlessly continuing to follow a path on which one embarked for other reasons—we have so many rules because in the Progressive and New Deal eras we created so many agencies, and agencies exist for the purpose of issuing these rules.

Regulation and Competition

The most insightful essay ever written about competition and its importance to markets was Hayek's "Competition as a Discovery Procedure."[5] Hayek's point was that only competition can discover the interests of consumers and how much they are willing to pay for a good or service. Although economists often speak about "perfect competition," what they don't recognize is that perfect competition is the result of a continuous price-discovery process. Markets, Hayek contends, are regulated by negative feedback. For example, before a product is introduced, the producer has no idea what the public will pay for it. If the price is set too high, the product may (perhaps) be sold profitably, but not as profitably as it could have been sold at a lower price and higher volume. This is often discovered by a competitor, who undercuts the original producer with an equivalent product at a lower price. The process continues until something like equilibrium is found at the price at which the last product sold—the marginal product—is sold at a profit, even though slight.

In other words, competition enables market participants to discover—temporarily—how much interest there is on the part of consumers and at what price level. The result is that, through relentless competition and free entry, the product is eventually produced at the lowest possible cost and sold at the lowest possible price. The process never really ends, because the existence of this product, whatever it is, changes the market for every other product—if only because product A absorbs some of the consumer funds that might have been spent on product B—in a never-ending loop. Equilibrium, then, is never really reached in a competitive and open market.

Government regulators and administrators would never have been able to simulate the market that Hayek describes, and at the same time it is obvious that the market will not function this way if regulation prevents it. "The most serious effect of government regulation on the market discovery process," writes Israel M. Kirzner in his 1985 book, "well might be the likelihood that regulation, in a variety of ways, may discourage, hamper, and even completely stifle the discovery process of the unregulated market."[6]

Every kind of regulation—licensure, minimum capitalization, minimum wages, or price controls of any kind—interfere with this process. At the very least, they impose compliance costs—people employed by producers to ensure that they are meeting the requirements of the rule—which must be included in prices and thus change the point at which the lowest cost may be discovered. This does not mean, of course, that these regulations are always inappropriate, but only that we should understand their costs in reduced competition and prices to consumers in relation to their benefits.

The kind of economic analysis known as public choice, which is discussed more fully later in this chapter, makes exactly this point:

Not very long ago, the simple proof that the economy did not function perfectly was regarded as an adequate reason for governmental action. Today, we start from the knowledge that the government also does not function perfectly and make a selection between two imperfect operational devices in terms of their relative perfection and certain other characteristics.... A deep-seated feeling that government is imperfect carries with it two consequences. The first is that imperfections in the market process do not necessarily call for government intervention; the second is a desire to see if we cannot do something about government processes that might conceivably improve their efficiency.[7]

One of the worst effects of regulation is to freeze industries—and sometimes markets—in place, erecting barriers to entry and requiring by regulation specific ways of carrying on a business. "The beneficent aspect of competition in the sense of a rivalrous process...arises out of freedom of entry," Kirzner notes. "What government regulations so often erect are regulatory barriers to entry. Freedom of 'entry' for the [Hayekian analyst] refers to the freedom of potential competitors to discover and to move to exploit existing opportunities for pure profit. If entry is blocked, such opportunities simply may never be discovered."[8]

A prime example is banking, a vibrant industry in the United States in the nineteenth and twentieth centuries, with as many as 25,000 banks competing nationally and locally (there are something like 6,500 today). To be sure, there were panics and failures, as there were in other industries, and of course during the Great Depression the banks were adversely affected by the restrictive monetary policies of the Federal Reserve. But two forms of regulation eventually killed the vibrancy of this industry—restrictions on interstate banking and deposit insurance. The first blocked freedom of entry so banks were not pressured by competition to become more efficient and were not able to diversify outside their localities in order to avoid local economic and financial downturns. The second factor, which was put in place because of the problems created by the first, gave the government control over bank products, operations, and capital levels.[9] Today, after the Dodd-Frank Act, there are few if any new banks being formed, the smaller community banks that are vital for local economic growth are gradually being driven to merge or close by expensive regulatory compliance costs, and the industry is dominated by four trillion-dollar giants. The chairman of one of these—JPMorgan Chase, an amalgam of many formerly independent New York banks— candidly acknowledged that regulation is a "moat" for his bank, keeping out competition from smaller institutions. The largest banks can spread regulatory costs across a broader asset base than can smaller banks, adding to their competitive advantages.

The regulatory costs of banking, however, are not the industry's only problem. Regulation, made necessary by deposit insurance, keeps commercial banks largely within the business of deposit taking and lending. When technology or other forms of innovation provide alternatives to deposit banking, the industry is unable to respond. For example, as shown in figure 5.3, the securities business—which allows investors to purchase debt securities issued by corporations—has become the dominant means of financing corporations in the United States. This occurred because changes in technology during the 1980s allowed companies to disseminate their financial information directly to potential investors, eliminating the information advantage once held by banks and providing a less expensive and more direct way for corporations to fund themselves.

It is interesting to consider whether we would have the robust securities industry we have today if, during the New Deal, Congress had decided to consolidate the regulation of securities and banks in a single agency. The precedent for this would have been the ICC's regulation of all the competing transportation modes. This turned out to be a destructive policy (discussed later in this chapter), as the ICC tried to balance and rationalize the competition between trucks and railroads for long-haul business. The result was to stifle competition, waste resources through inefficient operations, and impose higher costs on shippers and consumers. If the securities industry had been regulated by the regulator of banks, it is virtually certain that the industry would not have been allowed to grow as it has.

Another developing area of competition for banks is known as "fintech," firms intermediating between borrowers and lenders without the need for substantial amounts of capital. Again, this is a result of advances

FIGURE 5.3
Comparing Bank Commercial and Industrial Loans
with Corporate Debt Securities

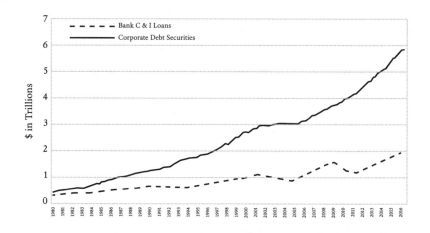

Source for debt securities: "Nonfinancial Corporate Business; Debt Securities; Liability, Level," FRED Economic Data, Federal Reserve Bank of St. Louis, https://fred.stlouisfed.org/series/NCBDBIQ027S (accessed April 18, 2018).

Source for business loans: "Commercial and Industrial Loans, All Commercial Banks," FRED Economic Data, Federal Reserve Bank of St. Louis, https://fred.stlouisfed.org/series/BUSLOANS (accessed April 18, 2018).

in communications technology that have made it possible for fintech firms to identify both borrowers and lenders virtually simultaneously and put the two together for a fee or commission. It is likely that the fintech idea, which is substantially less expensive than heavily regulated deposit banking, will also reduce the role of banks in the financial economy of the future. This will be painful for the banking industry, but ultimately good for consumers and the economy. And in due time, some innovation—perhaps arising in the banking industry if its regulators are flexible—will stunt the growth of fintech or supplant it entirely.

The Growth and Dollar Costs of Regulation

Federal agencies are required by Executive Order 12866, issued by President Bill Clinton in October 1993, to prepare a cost-benefit analysis for every "major" rule—defined as a rule having an economic impact of $100 million or more.[10] Before a major rule is issued, the agency's analysis is reviewed by OIRA (the Office of Information and Regulatory Affairs, an office within OMB). One has to be skeptical about this process; the agency issuing the rule has a lot at stake and is likely to have more information than OIRA about the effect of the rule. The analysis may not provide a complete picture, with the costs reduced and the benefits enlarged, and whether the rule will have a $100 million effect is always going to be debatable. If the agency turns out to be wrong, the penalty is not severe, if there is any penalty at all. Moreover, because of unforeseeable competitive changes in the industry caused by the regulation itself, the cost-benefit analysis that initially justified the rule may be wrong over the long term. The rule, however, remains in effect, and there is no routine mechanism for the government, including OIRA, to look back at how regulations are actually affecting those to whom they apply.

Even apart from its effects on competition, unnecessary regulation makes products and services more expensive than they might otherwise be, and thus adversely affects living standards, the availability of jobs, and the quality of life for most Americans. However, assessing the costs of regulations is exceedingly difficult because the U.S. government does virtually nothing to help scholars and others estimate these costs.[11] There is some irony here. One significant continuing cost that the government imposes on all businesses is reporting on economic and financial matters, enabling the government to assess how the economy is doing. This is useful and important, of course, but also important is what the government apparently does *not* want to know—the costs of the regulatory burdens, including the reporting burdens themselves, that the government has imposed on the private economy.

The effect of regulations on economic growth was dramatically illustrated with Donald Trump's election in November 2016. Trump had campaigned on a promise of regulatory relief, and almost immediately after his surprising win the U.S. stock markets began a sharp rise, which continued through his first year in office. This was well before Trump or the Republicans had formulated any tax or other legislation that might improve business conditions. There is no explanation for this other than that investors and the business community believed that Trump would appoint people to office who agreed with his deregulatory philosophy. Still, Paul Krugman, the *New York Times* columnist, fully reflected the conventional view of economists when he remarked, the day after the election, "If the question is when markets will recover, a first-pass answer is never."[12]

However, Trump's appointees to the cabinet and to other agencies seemed to be serious about reducing regulations, and through the first year of his presidency these officials provided many signals that regulation in their areas of control would be reduced. In July 2017 Trump announced that his administration had withdrawn or delayed at least eight hundred proposed rules that were under consideration when the Obama administration ended.[13] Actions like this were apparently enough to encourage the belief in the business community—for the first time since Barack Obama was elected—that the regulatory deluge would be reduced to a drizzle. Although few economists had noticed it, regulations were apparently so important in impeding growth that merely the prospect for reduced regulations was enough to prompt businesses to invest and hire new employees. This in itself is a demonstration that Crews's estimate of the regulatory burden on the U.S. economy—$2 trillion[14]—is close to accurate; there was a boom in 2017 well before taxes were cut, and right up until the end of 2017 the stock market was repeatedly hitting new highs even though passage of a significant tax cut was continually in jeopardy. The tax cut came at the very end of the year, but by then the U.S. economy had grown at almost a 3 percent pace, far outstripping the less than 2 percent growth rate during the highly regulatory Obama period.

The slow economic growth rate during the Obama administration was particularly unusual because it followed a deep recession that ended in June 2009. Normally, a sharp recovery follows a deep recession, but in the subsequent eight years the U.S. economy's growth of less than 2 percent was far below the growth rate of any previous period of recovery since the mid-1960s. The best explanation for this is the Dodd-Frank Act, discussed below, but it was also a period that included many other major regulatory initiatives—the net neutrality rule from the FCC, the fiduciary rule from the Labor Department, Operation Choke Point led by the Justice Department, and the mortgage rule issued by the CFPB. These reshaped (or threatened to reshape) whole industries. In addition, because the financial crisis was wrongly blamed on insufficient regulation of the financial system,[15] new banking rules raised the compliance costs of existing banks to such an extent that they impinged on lending to the small firms and startups that are the source of most economic growth and new employment in the United States. The formation of new banks during this period, which had been averaging a hundred per year before the financial crisis, was reduced to almost zero during Obama's eight years.

Other reasons for slow growth become clearer if we look at the Obama administration's major responses to the financial crisis, the recession, and the slow growth that followed. During this eight-year period, only four programs were significant enough to affect economic growth on their own: the Economic Recovery Act, which spent over $800 billion on supposedly "shovel-ready" projects; the Affordable Care Act, which poured money into the economy through health-care subsidies; and the Fed's quantitative easing (QE) program, which reduced interest rates to historic lows in an effort to spur business investment. If Keynesian spending actually does what its supporters claim, all of these policies should have stimulated substantial economic growth. It didn't happen. A major reason for this was the fourth major initiative, the Dodd-Frank Act, which was by far the most restrictive financial regulatory law since the New Deal. This law alone authorized almost four hundred new regulations of the financial system, many of which still had not been issued when the Obama administration ended. The connection between the Dodd-Frank Act and the slow growth that followed seems undeniable, and—given the substantial stimulative effort by the federal government—the fact that the economy could never get off the floor during the Obama years is an important indictment of regulation in general and the Dodd-Frank Act in particular.

Figure 5.4, a chart prepared by the Federal Reserve Bank of Dallas, shows the slow recovery of the economy from the 2008 financial crisis and ensuing recession as compared to the sharp recovery after virtually all other recessions since the 1960s.

All this indicates that regulatory costs are far more important than economists assume. Indeed, most economists do not seem to study regulation's effect on the economy at all, probably because there are no official or generally accepted nongovernmental numbers on regulatory costs. This is troubling, because in the absence of reliable data on regu-

FIGURE 5.4
The Slow Recovery from the 2008 Financial Crisis and the Ensuing Recession

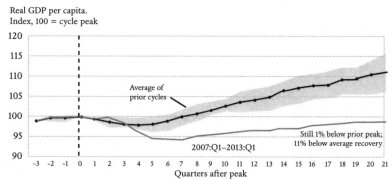

Real GDP per capita.
Index, 100 = cycle peak

Average of prior cycles

2007:Q1–2013:Q1

Still 1% below prior peak; 11% below average recovery

Quarters after peak

NOTE: The gray area indicates the range of major recessions since 1960, excluding the short 1980 recession.

Source: Tyler Atkinson, David Luttrell, and Harvey Rosenblum, "How Bad Was It?: The Costs and Consequences of the 2007–09 Financial Crisis," *Staff Papers*, Federal Reserve Bank of Dallas (July 2013), 4. https://www.dallasfed.org/~/media/documents/research/staff/staff1301.pdf. The authors' data comes from the Bureau of Economic Analysis, the Census Bureau, and their own calculations.

latory costs few policy makers grasp the effect that regulatory activities are having on the economy as a whole. Official reports then produce forecasts about economic growth that do not take into account the effect of existing and new regulations and thus cannot possibly be accurate. As a result, the government, Congress, the media, investors, and the public are all working with defective information about the economy, because they have no idea how regulation will affect economic growth, price levels, investment, and jobs in the future.

Accordingly, regulatory costs deserve serious study no matter how deficient the availability of information. It also means that the Trump administration, or any administration concerned with boosting economic growth, should take steps to provide the data that economists need to correlate regulation with economic growth. This is not to say that good estimates are not being made. The most comprehensive study of regulatory costs has been done annually by Crews, who, as noted, places the costs of regulations at close to $2 trillion,[16] exceeding the total of the individual and corporate income tax in 2016.

Crews has assembled this cost amount from a wide variety of

studies, private and governmental. The idea that a cost even remotely of this size would be completely ignored in estimating the direction of the economy is disturbing but somewhat understandable in light of the deficiencies in the data. The numbers, as even Crews admits, are squirrelly. It is wryly amusing, however, to see the great efforts that are made in Congress and among economists at the Congressional Budget Office to assess the effect of tax changes on the economy, while the agencies of the administrative state go merrily along—virtually unchallenged by anyone—imposing more and more invisible costs on the economy through regulation.

Although many agencies estimate the costs and benefits of their regulations, these estimates are not universally required or made, and they are almost never informed by cross-checking the agency's estimates with those of the individuals or firms actually regulated. Agencies have no incentive to do this, and sadly Congress has not seen fit to require any comprehensive study of regulatory costs. Cost-benefit analysis for individual regulations is not a substitute for a comprehensive study of all regulatory costs, based on data from firms that have to comply with the regulations. It is sad, but not surprising, that the government does not ask for this data when it places burdens on the private sector to report on their business activity. Somewhat more surprising is the fact that business associations do not routinely survey their members for the purpose of making cost estimates for particularly important regulations, let alone all the regulations that an industry might face. These associations should be developing information useful to policy makers that will reduce the adverse effect of government policies on their members.

Nevertheless, although the total regulatory costs to the economy are difficult to estimate, the actual numbers of regulations can be ascertained by counting what is published in the Federal Register, and these are distressing enough. According to Crews, there were 3,281 new regulations issued in 2017, somewhat less than the 3,297 in 2016. These 3,281 rules then joined the thousands of rules previously issued. Figure 5.5 shows the cumulative final rules issued by U.S. agencies and published in the Federal Register between 1993 and 2017.

A chart showing the cumulative growth of regulations is the right way to present this data. By and large, regulations do not go away after a

FIGURE 5.5

Cumulative Final Rules Published in the Federal Register, 1993–2017

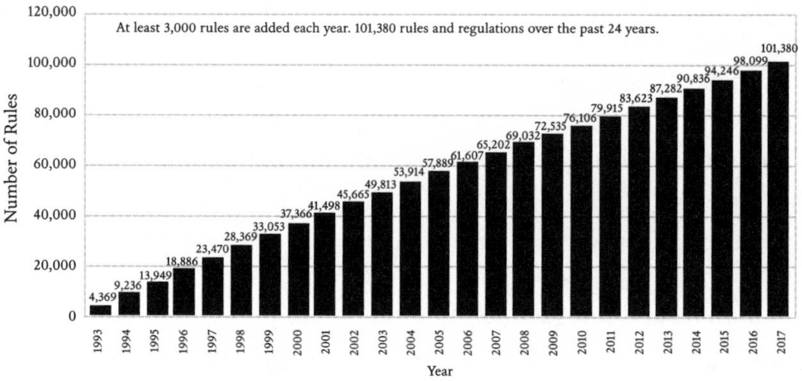

Source: Clyde Wayne Crews Jr., *Ten Thousand Commandments: An Annual Snapshot of the Federal Regulatory State—2018 Edition*, Competitive Enterprise Institute (April 19, 2018), Figure 13, https://cei.org/10kc2018. Crews's data comes from the National Archives and Records Administration, Office of the Federal Register.

while. The government does not take the trouble to repeal the ones that are no longer of use. They simply continue in effect, and are sometimes resurrected to do service when an agency encounters a new problem. The labor department is still issuing regulations under the Fair Labor Standards Act of 1938. Technically, then, a business may be subject to thousands of regulations that are now out of date and no longer enforced, but must still be on the agenda of diligent compliance officers because no one can be sure that the issuing agency will not enforce them someday. An unusual take on this phenomenon was published by the Mercatus Center in October 2017: "The US Code of Federal Regulations—the annually published set of books containing all federal regulations currently in effect—contained 35.4 million words in 1970.... By 2016, there were 104.6 million words of federal regulation on the books, about 195 percent growth over 1970."[17]

At the start of his administration, President Trump demanded that agencies repeal two regulations for every one they issue, but the graphic above does not show a substantial decline during 2017. However, as Crews points out, a substantial number of the regulations issued during 2017 were intended to be deregulatory but are still counted in the 2017 totals for final rules issued.

There have been useful efforts to consider the effect of regulatory costs on economic growth. One recent study, using as a baseline the regulations that were in place in 1980, found that the cumulative cost of regulations between 1980 and 2012 reduced economic growth in 2012 by 25 percent from what it would have been if no new regulations had been introduced after 1980. This amounted to nearly $13,000 per person in the United States in 2012.[18] The study shows that regulation can actually increase productivity in some cases, but the reduced growth computation came from netting increases and decreases across all industries. The authors conclude:

> The careful combination of modeling and data enables us to estimate the effects of regulation on investment in an endogenous growth context. In endogenous growth theory, innovation is not an exogenous gift from the gods but rather the result of costly effort expended by firms to realize gains. The growth generated by that entrepreneurship can be thwarted by misguided public policy. By deflecting firm resources away from the investments that maximize the stream of profits and toward regulatory compliance, regulations can theoretically slow the real growth of an industry.[19]

To wrap up this issue, it is useful to consider the Heritage Foundation's comprehensive and authoritative annual assessment of economic freedom in every country in the world. Assessments are based on twelve categories, including property rights, judicial effectiveness, tax burden, government spending, and business freedom, with regulations of business falling under the last category and not split out so that the effect of regulations is separately weighed. However, overall, the United States ranks seventeenth among all nations in economic freedom, and fifteenth in business freedom. According to the authors, the position of the United States declined between 2016 and 2017, recording its lowest overall economic freedom score ever and coming in below the United Arab Emirates, Chile, the United Kingdom, Georgia, and Lithuania, among many others.[20] The authors note:

> As successive editions of the *Index* have documented since 1995, the

affirmative link between economic freedom and long-term development is unmistakable and robust. Countries that allow their citizens more economic freedom achieve higher incomes and better standards of living. People in economically free societies have longer lives. They have better health and access to more effective education. They are able to be better stewards of the environment, and they push forward the frontiers of human achievement in science and technology through greater innovation.[21]

We already know, from looking around us, that the market today still does for consumers what Adam Smith noted in his time. Products and services are developed and sold in enormous variety and in a wide range of prices and quality, so as to be affordable to as many purchasers as possible. All this occurs through competition, which tends to drive down prices and increase quality, in most cases without any significant government regulation. Milton Friedman, as usual, describes it best:

> What the market does is to reduce greatly the range of issues that must be decided through political means, and thereby to minimize the extent to which government need participate directly in the game. The characteristic feature of action through political channels is that it tends to require or enforce substantial conformity. The great advantage of the market, on the other hand, is that it permits wide diversity.[22]

Diversity is only one of the benefits of a market economy. The fact that much of commercial life can go on without incident—mediated by the price system—is an indication that we should be asking for justifications whenever new regulations are proposed to address an economic problem. The first step should be to consider whether government intervention will be better than a private, market-based solution.

Initially, this seems difficult—the proponents of regulation can easily outline its immediate benefits, while its detriments are somewhat speculative. That's why Smith's observation is so important. From looking at how the economy works without regulation, it is clear that we will be giving up something significant if regulation is introduced. The question is whether the value of regulation exceeds the economic growth, innovation, and efficiency we have to sacrifice.

Questions about Regulation: Ronald Coase and the Public Choice Theorists

The standard explanation for economic regulation is "market failure"—that the market's normal functioning, in which exchanges like those of Adam Smith with his butcher and brewer take place, is flawed in some respect. For example, there were parties to the transaction, or outside it, that were harmed in some way and could not be compensated through the pricing system. Many of these parties—say, the family that lived across the street from the brewer—had to live with the smells and noises emanating from the brewing process but received no compensation from the brewer. In the idealized situation described in this case, the government might step in by requiring the brewer to install equipment that would suppress the noise and odor. This section will be concerned with the question of "market failure" and whether the theory that largely justifies regulation can withstand analysis.

The classic case—where the odors and noises from a brewery disrupt the quiet enjoyment of their property by those who live near it—tests the necessity for regulation. Many economists and regulators would argue that this reflects a market failure; there is no way, they contend, that the market can compensate those who live near the brewery for their loss, so the government should adopt regulations that require the brewery to "internalize" the costs it is creating for those who live around it. This can be done in two ways—through a tax that is reduced when the brewery installs equipment that reduces the odors, or through regulation that requires the brewery to install the equipment as a price of continuing its operations.

Ronald Coase was one of the first to call into question the validity of the assumption underlying much of modern regulation—that the only way to rectify the brewer-homeowner problem is through government action. As he points out in his seminal paper, "The Problem of Social Cost," the first reaction—to restrain A (in this case, the brewer)—is wrong. As he sees it, the real problem is "to avoid more serious harm."

Coase first points out that, in the common law of nuisance, as it developed initially in England, both parties—the brewer and the homeowner—were seen as having some responsibility for a given nuisance problem. The brewer might be creating noxious odors, but the homeowner could live elsewhere, and there is a price at which the troubled homeowner would be willing to settle the matter. If the brewer will pay that price, the homeowner and the brewer will have settled the issue between themselves, without the need for a regulation. Coase points out that welfare economists—those who see market failures that cannot be mediated by the pricing system—would force the brewer to install some controls. This might solve the homeowner's problem, but in Coase's analysis it is the wrong solution because it imposes social costs.

When social cost—the effect on the community as a whole—is considered, a regulation requiring the brewer to pay a tax or install odor-suppressing equipment turns out to be a burden on the users of the brewer's products, who face higher costs. They, in effect, are paying a cost to benefit the homeowners who live near the brewery. Instead, a private settlement between the brewer and the homeowner—with the brewer paying the affected homeowners what they believe is a fair price for enduring the odors the brewer is creating—would be less costly for the rest of society than a regulation or a tax. Coase points out that the common law of nuisance achieved exactly this kind of solution, compensating those who were actually injured, without imposing large additional costs on society at large. "The problem," he says, "is to devise practical arrangements which will correct defects in one part of the system without causing more serious harm in other parts."[23]

Welfare economists, Coase observes, fail to recognize that their solutions have social costs that they do not take into account. Even if a tax or regulation could be devised that would exactly compensate the neighbors of a factory against the smoke that it emits, it would not solve the problem of social cost:

> Even if the tax is exactly adjusted to equal the damage that would be done to neighboring properties as a result of the emission of each additional puff of smoke, the tax would not necessarily bring about optimal conditions. An increase in the number of people living or

of business operating in the vicinity of the smoke-emitting factory will increase the amount of harm produced by a given emission of smoke. The tax that would be imposed would therefore increase with an increase in the number of those in the vicinity. This will tend to lead to a decrease in the value of production of the factors employed by the factory.... But people deciding to establish themselves in the vicinity of the factory [because of the decreased smoke] *will not take into account this fall in the value of production which results from their presence.*[24]

This analysis obviously raises questions about the efficacy of regulation in general—whether it is the most sensible way to address a problem. As in the English law of nuisance, the affected parties can often work out a better result through the pricing system. It goes back to the observation initially made by Adam Smith, that in a private transaction everyone gets what he wants, and there would not be a transaction unless that were true.

Government intervention can have far-reaching effects through ill-considered social costs that make the solution, from a social standpoint, worse than the problem that it was created to solve. This in itself can explain why regulation can have—and may in fact be having—such an adverse effect on economic growth in the United States. In addition, if a regulation is for some reason unavoidable, have its social costs been adequately accounted for? This is more subtle than a simple cost-benefit analysis. What Coase is suggesting is that the productivity losses in the same or other industries—jobs lost, businesses closed, consumer costs increased, and adverse international trade effects—should be considered before it is clear that a particular regulation makes sense from a social perspective. This obviously goes well beyond the kind of cost-benefit analysis that many view as necessary for new regulations, and adds weight to the cost side of the ledger that is seldom considered.

Public Choice Theory

Coase is not the only critic of welfare economics and the value of regulation. James Buchanan and Gordon Tullock, among others, attack it from another standpoint: public choice theory. Buchanan received a Nobel Prize in 1986 for his work in this area. Again, the critique begins with the point that when two people transact both of them "win." But public choice contests the view that government action is better than private bargaining because government officials are selfless and motivated by the public interest rather than profit. Thus, in an essay first published in 1988, Geoffrey Brennan and Buchanan write:

> Although we do not believe that narrow self-interest is the *sole* motive of political agents, or that it is necessarily as relevant a motive in political as in market settings, we certainly believe it to be a significant motive. This differentiates our approach from the alternative model, implicit in conventional welfare economics and widespread in conventional political science, that political agents can be satisfactorily modeled as motivated solely to promote the "public interest," somehow conceived. *That* model we, along with all our public choice colleagues, categorically reject.[25]

Instead of a theory of "market failure," as used by the welfare economists, public choice adherents posit a theory of "government failure." Public choice theory, Buchanan notes, "contains demonstrations that observed political-government processes fail to satisfy the requirements for efficiency [in achieving a beneficial result] in the implementation of corrective measures."[26] The reason for this is that government officials, like private individuals, pursue their self-interest, not the public interest. Buchanan observes:

> The central methodological thrust of Public Choice is the extension of straightforward utility-maximization to explain the behavior of persons who act in public-choice roles. Voters, bureaucrats, judges, legislators—these roles are filled by persons much like everyone else who seek to maximize their own utilities, subject to the constraints (rules) within which they operate.... If bureaucratic rewards generally depend on size of agency, which in turn depends on the size of agency budgets, supervisors of bureaus will seek to maximize budget sizes, quite independently of any "demand" for the services actually

provided. Unlike the owners of a private firm, bureaucrats are unable to capture rents or profits directly. They, therefore, seek to expand agency size beyond meaningful efficiency limits.[27]

Needless to say, the regulations adopted by self-interested public officials are not likely to produce good results for society; they are more likely to have been developed and promulgated for the purpose of increasing the power—or the sense of power—of the officials who wrote them than to correct the problems they were purportedly attempting to address. In chapter 4, on Progressivism, I note that Frankfurter and other Progressives were disappointed with the work of the regulatory agencies in which they had placed so much trust. This would not have surprised public choice theorists, who thought that government failure is more likely than private failure, and when government failure occurs it is more pervasive and costly than market failure.

In addition, as distinguished from using the pricing system for private settlement of so-called market failures, public choice theory says that government regulation is likely to be contrary to the interests and desires of large portions of the public. This is because, when the government acts, it chooses a solution that is acceptable to a majority coalition of the polity in which it is operating and then coerces the minority to conform. Public choice theory thus explains the effect of regulations in reducing freedom of choice for Americans. All regulations, even those actually consistent with what Congress has authorized, are made on behalf of a coalition that does not include a minority of the country.

This does not make the regulation wrong—the purpose of Congress is to make these decisions even though they override the interests of a minority—but it does call into question whether regulations are always the best way to resolve a societal problem. For this reason, public choice theory favors limited government action and a constitutional system that limits the power of the government to impose rules. But an additional dimension is based on the likelihood that the government officials who are imposing a rule—especially a rule that goes beyond what Congress intended—are acting in their own interests and not necessarily in the interests of the public.

Thus Buchanan notes that, "once politics was discovered as the apparent low-cost means of imposing preferences on behavior, a Pandora's box was opened that shows no signs of closing itself.... In democracy, politicians respond to the electorates, and electoral majorities may, in piecemeal fashion, close off one liberty after another." And he cautions: "Until and unless we recognize that politics, too, must operate within constitutional limits, each of our liberties, whether valued highly or slightly, is up for grabs."[28] Accordingly, public choice adherents would favor a system in which checks and balances prevent the government from acting too easily to adopt regulations, and thus would support the thesis of this book that much unnecessary regulation could be avoided if courts took a more careful look at whether administrative agencies are acting within the authorities granted by Congress or are instead acting in their own interests.

There are other criticisms of excessive regulation. Christopher De-Muth, director of OIRA in the Reagan administration, points out that "executive government disconnects law from the deliberations, compromises, and parochial concerns of the representative legislature. It is more likely than legislation to go to extremes, because...it is specialized and the product of insular subcultures of agencies and their 'stakeholders.'" Moreover, if the limits on Congress's ability to delegate authority to specialized agencies are reduced or eliminated, it "produces too much law. This is not to say that Congress is more inclined than agencies to adhere to the teachings of classic liberalism; rather, the sheer pertinacity of the modern administrative state inevitably penetrates and politicizes many areas of life better left to economic markets, social norms, private institutions, and personal judgments."[29]

Regulation, Freedom to Act, and Economic Growth

If it is even partially correct that the social costs of regulation are frequently negative, that regulation is often imposed for the benefit of officials rather than the public, and that regulation impairs economic growth, we should expect to find productivity improvement and other economic benefits when industries are relieved of regulation—and that is exactly what we do see in the rare cases where government regulation has actually been reduced.

In the mid-1970s and early 1980s, a movement to reduce economic regulation was led by Alfred Kahn, an economist who was the chairman of the Civil Aeronautics Board during the Carter administration. The CAB was responsible for airline rate and route regulation; under its control, fares were high, investment was low, and services on many routes outside the major cities were limited. The airlines competed mostly through perquisites like meals, seating, and other benefits for the business passengers who were their primary customers.

In 1978, however, during Kahn's CAB chairmanship and with his encouragement and support, Congress enacted the Airline Deregulation Act, which eliminated the CAB and its rate and route regulation. This extraordinary act, in which an agency head actually supported the abolition of his agency, was described in 2012 as "one of the greatest microeconomic policy accomplishments of the past fifty years.... It was the first dismantling of a substantial economic regulatory apparatus, and one of the only instances that included abolition of the relevant regulatory agency."[30] The successful deregulation of the airlines was a "compelling demonstration of the benefits of replacing regulation with competition [and it] advanced a broader reform agenda, both in the United States and abroad. 'Without airline deregulation...we probably would not have been able...to deregulate trucking, railroads, and buses, or continue along the same path with other major industries.'"[31] Today, anyone who flies regularly in the United States sees whole families going to visit Grandma because of the low cost of flights, and a system of trunk lines and secondary lines that get passengers almost anywhere in the country in a day. There are service complaints, to be sure, but in 2016, U.S. airlines carried nearly one billion passengers to U.S. and foreign destinations.

In the late 1970s, railroads, trucks, buses, and even barges reflected the same capital investment and efficiency problems as the airline industry. Accordingly, in 1980 Congress adopted the Staggers Rail Act—again with the support of an economist who was the chair of the relevant regulator, the Interstate Commerce Commission. This law substantially deregulated the railroad industry. A companion law, the Motor Carrier Act of 1980, commensurately reduced the power of the ICC to set rates, routes, and other standards for trucks that competed with the railroads. The ICC had been established as the first independent regulatory agency in 1887, and first regulated only the railroads. As trucks, buses, and other modes of carriage were added as competitors for the railroads, Congress handed their regulation over to the ICC. Again, as in the case of the airlines, inefficiencies reigned; trucks, for example, were unable to carry return loads after making a delivery because that was deemed to be unfair competition for the railroads. Investment, productivity, and innovation were seriously lagging in all the transportation modes regulated by the ICC.

The Staggers Act changed all that. The Federal Railroad Administration concluded that the removal of a good number of regulatory restraints provided "the industry increased flexibility to adjust their rates and tailor services to meet shipper needs and their own revenue requirements. As a result, 30 years after deregulation, the railroad industry's financial health has improved significantly, service to rail customers has improved while overall rates have decreased, and rail safety, regardless of the measure, has improved."[32]

Deregulation also worked for trucking, the biggest competitor for railroads. The Motor Carrier Act of 1980 was enacted over the objections of the trucking industry and the teamsters, substantially freeing the trucking industry from regulation by the ICC. This, too, resulted in major improvements in rates and services:

> Between 1977, the year before the ICC started to decontrol the industry, and 1982, rates for truckload-size shipments fell about 25 percent in real, inflation-adjusted terms. The General Accounting Office found that rates charged by LTL (less-than-truckload) carriers had fallen as much as 10 to 20 percent, with some shippers reporting declines of as much as 40 percent.... A survey of shippers indicates that they believe service quality improved as well.... Shippers reported that carriers were much more willing to negotiate rates and services than prior to deregulation.[33]

An MIT study concluded the same in 2013: "Trucking output has more than doubled in the 30 years after deregulation, and today trucking is perhaps the most dominant mode of freight transportation. These developments owe much to the increased competitiveness of trucking, the ascendancy of intermodal transportation, and shifts in transported commodities toward smaller, high value items."[34]

Other deregulation activities occurred in the 1970s and 1980s. Fixed commissions on securities trading were abolished by Congress in 1975, spawning a whole new business of discount brokerage. The cost of trading securities fell precipitously, and many more Americans became investors because of the reduced cost of buying and selling securities. As one observer of Wall Street noted, the end of fixed commissions "smashed Wall Street's monopoly, unleashing the discount-brokerage industry, fostering independent research and democratizing the world of investing."[35] Today, shares can be bought and sold for pennies. In addition, shortly after becoming president, Ronald Reagan deregulated oil and gasoline prices, putting an end to the shortages and gas lines that plagued the country during the 1970s. It is worth noting that, in all of these cases, there was strong opposition to deregulation by various groups, often by consumer advocates and the regulated industry itself. But in all cases, after deregulation the market functioned better, generally with lower prices and greater availability of products and services, than it did before.

Net Neutrality

Can we expect regulation to have the same effect if it is introduced into markets where it has not previously existed? This is the principal issue in the so-called net neutrality controversy, a case in which the government has sought to impose more regulation on the internet, a market that had been innovating and developing effectively without regulation for more than twenty-five years. Indeed, over that period, without any government support and with minimal regulatory intervention, the internet had blossomed into an essential element of the U.S. and world economy.

Nevertheless, during the Obama administration, under pressure from the president himself, the FCC adopted a policy called net neutrality, which (among other things) requires the organizations that transmit messages and data, known as internet service providers (ISPs), to charge the same rates for all internet usage, and not to prefer one user over another. In other words, ISPs were to be treated as common carriers—like point-to-point telephone service—under the Telecommunications Act of 1996.

This was new. Normally, the reasons for political pressure in favor of regulation are based on allegations of some form of abuse of the public— ordinarily cited as a market failure. For example, the Interstate Commerce Commission was established in 1887 in the wake of complaints by farmers that they were subject to discriminatory railroad rates. But the pressure for net neutrality was not based on any significant degree of discriminatory or antitrust activity by ISPs; instead, it was based on the idea that ISPs had sufficient market power to impose discriminatory rates and service requirements in the future, even though there was very little evidence that they had ever done so.

In reality, almost all the evidence was on the other side. As Bruce Owen wrote in a 2015 policy brief for the Stanford Institute for Economic Policy Research, the ISP industry "has been the focus of rapid technological change characterized by movement from analog to digital transmission, from fixed to mobile service and from lower to higher speeds or bandwidths." This has resulted in an increase in "the number of alternative providers available to most households. While it is always possible that various threats to competition and economic efficiency may arise down the road, there is little current evidence to support a call for [net neutrality] regulation."[36]

Fortunately, in 2017, under a new president and a new FCC chairman, the FCC began a process to repeal the net neutrality regulation the agency had adopted. Its statement of reasons included the following: "The Commission's [net neutrality] order has put at risk online investment and innovation, threatening the very open Internet it purported to preserve. Investment in broadband networks declined. Internet service providers have pulled back on plans to deploy new and upgraded infrastructure and services to consumers."[37]

As this statement suggests, the spur of competition in the nonregulated ISP industry has produced a substantial amount of innovation by ISPs in a little over twenty-five years. Net neutrality, which would prohibit differential rates for internet users, would bring this innovation to a halt. To cite only one example, why would any ISP make investments that would produce higher internet speeds in the future if it could not recover the cost of that innovation through higher rates from those who would benefit most from the higher speeds? This is the way almost all innovation works, if it involves a substantial investment by the provider. To justify the cost of putting the innovation into effect, the provider wants to be as certain as possible that there are likely to be customers for the product or service, and the first customers are those who are willing to pay the costs of using the innovation because it provides them with a competitive advantage or avoids a competitive disadvantage. Once the innovation is in place, and its costs of initial implementation are recovered, the continuing costs fall sharply over time because of new competition entering the market, making it available to all users. Without the incentive to invest, innovation won't happen, and the innovation that has characterized the U.S. internet to date will grind to a halt.

The Progressive mindset will probably always be with us. More than anything else, it reflects a lack of understanding of how the market works and thus an inability to imagine how competition—through what economist Joseph Schumpeter called "creative destruction"—can do a better job than the government can of regulating a market. There is no better example of this than the latter-day progressives' demand for net neutrality.

Regulation Has a Better Reputation Than It Deserves

As this chapter makes clear, though regulation is so common we accept it as a matter of course, it has many flaws. "The entrenched administrative state," writes Richard Epstein, "especially on issues of fair competition and price stability, causes real economic loss and social dislocation precisely because it hobbles the dynamic elements of markets."[38] Studies show that its costs to the U.S. economy rival taxation, yet the growth of regulation is seldom taken into account by macroeconomists who study the economy's performance. As a result, as Ronald Coase points out, it is likely to be a poor substitute for the price system in resolving disputes, and its principal proponents frequently fail to understand or take account of the social costs it imposes.

In addition, regulation is based in part on the idea that regulators are selfless and public spirited, whereas public choice theorists make a strong case that government officials are motivated by self-interest like everyone else, and point out that regulations unnecessarily impose the views of a governing coalition when private forms of conflict resolution would be fairer and work better. In the few cases where regulation has actually been eliminated, the market has functioned well, reducing costs and increasing investment. This appears to confirm that competition in the right circumstances can be a better economic regulator than the government.

Accordingly, there are strong policy grounds for much more skepticism about the efficacy of regulation than has shaped thinking since the New Deal—and indeed since the Progressive Era. Congress should resist the temptation to adopt legislation that authorizes new regulatory burdens on the private sector, and the judiciary should show less receptivity to and support for regulations that do not have a strong foundation in the language Congress actually adopted. Adopting such a mindset in the legislative and judicial branches would both foster economic growth and bring a return to the system of checks and balances that the Framers envisioned as a necessary means to preserve the liberties of the American people.

6

===

THE NONDELEGATION DOCTRINE

Chevron importantly guards against the Judiciary arrogating to itself policymaking properly left, under the separation of powers, to the Executive. But there is another concern at play, no less firmly rooted in our constitutional structure. That is the obligation of the Judiciary not only to confine itself to its proper role, but to ensure that the other branches do so as well.

CHIEF JUSTICE JOHN ROBERTS[1]

Article I of the Constitution provides that "All legislative Powers herein granted shall be vested in a Congress of the United States, which shall consist of a Senate and House of Representatives." This simple yet definitive phrasing means that Congress alone within the U.S. government has the power to make the laws. But law—a system of government-made rules that, if violated, will subject a private party (a person or an entity) to criminal prosecution or civil liability—is broader than legislation. By that definition, a rule issued by an administrative agency is a law, and administrative rules are made by agencies that are part of the executive branch, not Congress. What, then, has become of the Constitution's statement that only Congress has the power to legislate?

The beginning of analysis is to understand the difference between a legislature and an administrative agency. A legislature is a unique body. Its decisions, unless they are in conflict with a constitution, cannot be overturned because they are unfair, discriminatory, or not based on evidence. The distinguishing feature of legislation is that it has an *ipse dixit* (because I said so) character; it is arbitrary and wholly discretionary. This enables a legislature like the U.S. Congress to make the major—and difficult—policy choices for society, favoring the interests of some and disfavoring the interests of others. These legislative decisions authorize the president and the administrative agencies of the executive branch to make subordinate rules that fill in the details of the legislation.

Because it is not a legislature, an administrative agency cannot be arbitrary and wholly discretionary; it must act on the basis of evidence, and it must act within the four corners of the congressional legislation that provides its authority. Concerns about the growth of the administrative state arise because it appears to many Americans that administrative agencies, and not Congress, are making the major policy choices that should belong to Congress. This is of concern not merely because the Constitution gave Congress alone the legislative power of the government, but more particularly because Congress, elected by the American people, is representative of the people and administrative agencies are not.

Because of the exclusive nature of the Constitution's grant to Congress—"all legislative power"—many legal scholars, judges, and others have argued that it is a violation of the Constitution for Congress to transfer (or delegate) any of its legislative authority to administrative agencies or others, and that any such delegation should be declared unconstitutional by the courts.[2] This is the so-called nondelegation doctrine.

However, other scholars—reprising the arguments of the Progressives—contend that, in an era more complex than when the Constitution was designed, Congress cannot avoid delegating legislative authority. Instead, for example, it should simply choose the agency that will carry out the delegated legislative function.[3] Still others, assuming that the need for delegation of legislative authority is indisputable, argue that "the administrative state is now constitutionally obligatory, rendered necessary by the reality of delegation."[4]

These are arguments for practicality, or facing "reality" as some see it, but it is important to understand that those who take this position must be willing to allow administrative agencies—instead of Congress—to make the major choices for society. There is very little evidence today that this is necessary. During the Progressive Era and the New Deal, the problems facing the country were unprecedented; it was rational to believe that only the government could solve them. That can no longer be confidently asserted. The government's many failures during and since these periods—some of them outlined in the previous chapter—require, at the least, substantial evidence that the constitutional structure designed by the Framers is unable to manage the country's problems today. In the absence of such evidence, it cannot be the right decision to turn over the power to make the choices for society to the unelected agencies of the administrative state. It would be an abandonment of the Constitution as well as a betrayal of democracy.

In this chapter, I also show that the separation of powers, as conceived by the Framers, cannot work unless the courts are willing to invoke the nondelegation doctrine in appropriate cases.

Why Is the Nondelegation Doctrine Important?

At the most fundamental level, the nondelegation doctrine protects and preserves the role of Congress, as a legislature, to make the most important decisions for society. If Congress were permitted to delegate its exclusive legislative authority to the administrative agencies in the executive branch, the separation of powers would be a nullity and the dangers to liberty envisioned by the Framers could become a reality. Allowing the legislative authority of Congress to move formally or informally into the hands of the administrative agencies of the executive branch would also mean the end of our democracy, as the major decisions for society would no longer be made by the representatives of the American people but by the unelected bureaucracies of the administrative state.

The claim by supporters of the administrative state that the president, an elected and accountable person, would then be making these decisions is feeble and inconsistent with the separation of powers. If the matter is legislative in nature, it must be decided by Congress; if it is a subordinate issue—filling in the details—it can be done by the administrative agency without consulting or involving the president. In other words, a connection to the president is irrelevant as a constitutional matter. In any event, the president has limited control over the rulemaking by agencies of the executive branch, and is mostly unable to control the regulatory policies they pursue. As Chief Justice Roberts observed in his *City of Arlington* dissent: "Although the Constitution empowers the President to keep federal officers accountable, administrative agencies enjoy in practice a significant degree of independence." Then, quoting an article by Elena Kagan before she joined the Court, he continued: "no president (or his executive office staff) could, and presumably none would wish to, supervise so broad a swath of regulatory activity."[5] Even the Trump administration, which has made it a priority to cut back on regulation, had only a limited effect in 2017, and seems to be headed for an increase in regulations in 2018. Indeed, the five most active rulemaking agencies, once again in 2018, were executive departments headed by appointees who report directly to the president. As Wayne Crews notes, "the problem of overregulation is largely driven by entrenched delegation of rule-making power to agencies by Congress."[6]

Both the structure of the Constitution and the way it was approved by the American people argue in favor of the nondelegation doctrine. As conceived at the time it was written, the Constitution was a compact among the people of the states that approved it. Following the ideas of John Locke in his *Second Treatise of Government*, the Framers believed that by approving the Constitution the American people had transferred or delegated to the government their inherent and natural right to govern themselves, and in particular the right to create the laws under which all of them would live. Congress, as the representative body created by the Constitution, was the repository of those inherent rights.

This compact imposes a restriction on further delegation by Congress. In common law countries like the United States, when a principal delegates its authority to an agent, the agent cannot subdelegate that authority to anyone without the principal's approval. This is entirely logical, because the principal is relying on the faithful service of the agent, and a subdelegation to someone else entails the risk that the subagent will not faithfully carry out the principal's directions. Thus, because the American people, in approving the Constitution, delegated their inherent law-making power to Congress, this authority cannot be delegated to anyone else without the approval of the American people expressed through an amendment of the Constitution.

Leaving aside this theoretical way of describing the delegation issue, there is the logic of the separation of powers principle. The Constitution divided all governmental powers among a legislature, an executive, and a judiciary, because the Framers—and presumably the American people who ratified the Constitution—believed that the only effective way to preserve liberty over the long run was to separate these powers from one another. In *Federalist* No. 47, Madison states that, if all these powers were combined in the same person or group, that would be the "very definition of tyranny." Accordingly, if it is dangerous to combine legislative power with executive power, it would be equally dangerous for the legislature to delegate its powers to the executive branch.

Recent events have demonstrated that Madison did not wildly overstate his case. As described in chapter 1, a Justice Department initiative called Operation Choke Point, carried out by the Obama administration, was precisely the combination of legislative and executive power that the Framers feared. Using the existing legal authority of bank regulators, Operation Choke Point sought to deprive payday lenders—a lawful business but one disfavored by the Obama administration—of financial support. Fortunately for the companies involved, and ultimately the rule of law, a court—as the Framers intended—correctly used its independent power to determine that the effort was a violation of law and the Constitution.

These facts make clear that it is essential, even today, to preserve the separation of powers by preserving the nondelegation doctrine. Not only would this protect against future government actions that might threaten American liberties, but it would also assure that only Congress will make the major governing decisions for the American people.

The judiciary's important role in this process is made more urgent today than in the past because of the substantial decline in the power and independence of Congress since the New Deal. As described in chapter 3, the political party system has reduced the interest of Congress in maintaining its independence from the president—especially when one party controls both chambers of Congress and the presidency. Also outlined in chapter 3 are the strong incentives for Congress to avoid the difficult task of legislating. By its nature, legislation requires Congress to make difficult choices among contending groups, and puts individual members in jeopardy of defeat in the next election. The fact that the Supreme Court, under *Chevron*, has given administrative agencies great latitude in interpreting their own authority is also a factor; *Chevron* deference raises a legitimate question as to whether Congress should spend so much time and effort negotiating the words of a statute when administrative agencies are able to reinterpret the statutory language to broaden their authority beyond what Congress intended to provide. Finally, and perhaps most important, Congress has increasingly found that its members will get political credit from voters—and little voter opposition—if they simply authorize an administrative agency to achieve a goal of some kind, without the trouble of settling on who should bear the cost of doing so.

Because of these factors, unless the courts actually *require* Congress to make legislative decisions—by reviving and implementing the nondelegation doctrine—Congress is likely to slide increasingly into the mode of setting goals and handing increasing amounts of authority to administrative agencies. If that occurs, even the willingness of the courts to determine "what the law is" through judicial review will not prevent power from moving inexorably to the agencies of the administrative state. For example, if Congress authorizes an agency to achieve a goal, and sets no other standards, there is nothing for a court to decide in the judicial review process. On the other hand, if the courts begin to take the nondelegation doctrine seriously, and declare one or more of these delegations invalid, it will force Congress to make the difficult decisions that it is required to make as a legislature in the constitutional structure.

What seems clear, then, is that unless the courts develop a nondelegation jurisprudence, forcing Congress to do the difficult work of legislating, we are headed ultimately for a form of government in which a bureaucracy in Washington—and not Congress—will make the major policy decisions for the country.

The Courts and the Nondelegation Doctrine

Unfortunately, in the 230 years since the ratification of the Constitution, the courts have made little progress in developing a jurisprudence of nondelegation. Whatever the reason—lack of fortitude, adherence to precedent, or a misplaced concern about interfering with the elected branches—the courts have not made clear to Congress that delegations of legislative authority would not be permitted.

This is troubling, because the Framers thought of the judiciary as one of the key elements of the checks and balances structure they had built into the Constitution. Bolstered by the life tenure of its members, the judiciary was ideally suited to prevent action or inaction by one of the other branches from eroding the constitutional structure. If, for example, Congress failed to defend its powers against encroachments by the executive, the judiciary would step in to restore the intended balance. This was also to occur if the executive assumed powers that Congress had not granted—something that occurred, famously, in 1948, when the Supreme Court struck down President Harry Truman's seizure of the steel mills, and in 2015, when the courts stopped President Obama's suspension of the immigration laws. Nevertheless, as Congress has gradually ceded more and more authority to administrative agencies since the New Deal, the courts have been unwilling to raise the nondelegation doctrine as an issue, and counsel for affected litigants have increasingly come to believe that the doctrine is no longer worth presenting to a court in an appropriate case.

This should not be surprising. Although it has not been formally abandoned, the Supreme Court has not invoked the nondelegation doctrine since 1935. The two cases decided that year—*Panama Refining* and *Schechter*—were based on sound reasoning by the Court, but have not been followed in the more than eighty years since. This has raised a legitimate question of the doctrine's continuing validity, and many legal scholars consider it effectively dead.

Indeed, the Supreme Court has gone the other way, holding in *Chevron v. Natural Resources Defense Council*, in 1984, that courts should generally defer to an agency's interpretation of its own statutory authority, if that interpretation is "reasonable." This decision, described more fully in chapter 7, substantially increased the authority of administrative agencies, especially in cases in which Congress has not specifically defined the scope of their powers. For this reason, *Chevron* is the Supreme Court decision that is most responsible for the growth of the administrative state, as well as the decision that raises the most important questions about the continued viability of the nondelegation doctrine.

The difficulty of defining the line between legislation and administration should not be minimized. It can be done, however, if the courts are willing to think about and describe what is—and what is not—a legislative act. Courts often take on these definitional burdens, as when they define the scope of "interstate commerce," the meaning of an unlawful "search and seizure," or address dozens of other issues arising under the Constitution's necessarily general language. Defining the line between legislation and administration is arguably even more important, however, because it addresses not merely the Constitution's words but its fundamental structure.

As early as 1825, in *Wayman v. Southard*, Chief Justice Marshall faced the problem of distinguishing between the power of Congress to enact legislation and the authority of an agency to administer the law Congress enacted. In this case, the issue before the Court was whether Congress, in the Judiciary Act of 1789, had improperly delegated to the judiciary the authority for processing certain cases. Marshall, writing for the Court, concluded that Congress could delegate to others decisions that would otherwise be within its jurisdiction but were actually minor or unimportant:

> It will not be contended that Congress can delegate to the courts or to any other tribunals powers which are strictly and exclusively *legislative*. But Congress may certainly delegate to others powers which the legislature may rightfully exercise itself.... The courts, for example, may make rules directing the returning of writs and processes...and other things of the same description. It will not be contended that these things might not be done by the legislature...yet it is not alleged that the power may not be conferred on the Judicial Department.
>
> The line has not been exactly drawn which separates *those important subjects* which must be *entirely regulated by the legislature itself* from those of *less interest* in which a general provision may be

made and power given to those who are to act under such general
provisions to fill up the details....

The power given to the Court to vary the mode of proceeding
in this particular is a power to vary *minor regulations* which are
within the *great outlines marked out by the legislature in directing the
execution.*[7]

Thus, in a few sentences, Chief Justice Marshall laid out a viable—if
difficult—standard for determining the difference between legislation
and administration. Legislation, he said, consists of "important" items,
but Congress can delegate the unimportant items. At first this idea seems
circular, but Marshall added that the delegation must take place within
the "great outlines marked out" by Congress. The opinion thus moved
the inquiry from what is "legislation" to what is an "important" decision,
and Marshall suggests that at least one definition of an important decision is that it marks out a limited territory within which a subordinate
agency is authorized to act.

As Marshall suggested, a statute embodies the major policy decisions
of Congress and may leave lesser decisions to agencies like the Treasury
Department or the Environmental Protection Agency. These lesser decisions may also be important in some sense, but whether a particular
issue left to the judgment of an administrative agency is an "important"
policy decision that should have been made by Congress—or is merely
the filling in of details—is a judgment for a court. In *Wayman*, as Marshall saw it, delegating decisions within a "great outline" marked out by
the legislature would be sufficient.

The fact that Chief Justice Marshall, as early as 1825, was required to
consider the difference between legislation and administration demonstrates that this issue is inherent in the separation of powers and not
an artifact of the more complex society and governmental system we
have today. From the early days of the country, Congress established
major cabinet-level departments, such as Treasury, State, and War, and
authorized them to take certain actions on behalf of the government. The
Framers surely knew that in separating legislative and executive powers
they had left the difficult issue of distinguishing between legislative and

administrative actions for the judiciary to arbitrate in the future. That is one of the reasons that Hamilton argued in *Federalist* No. 78 that the judges needed life tenure: they would be taking on the more powerful elected branches. Unfortunately, the judiciary has not embraced this responsibility with enthusiasm.

The Supreme Court and the Nondelegation Doctrine

The nondelegation doctrine is so fundamental to retaining both the separation of powers and the checks and balances system that one would expect it to get serious and frequent attention from the courts. However, there have been relatively few cases in which the doctrine has been raised and discussed at the Supreme Court, and until 1935 the Court had never found a case in which an unconstitutional delegation of legislative authority occurred. One of the reasons for this might be the overwhelming power of Congress within the constitutional system—a power noted ruefully by Woodrow Wilson during the Progressive Era. Until quite late in the nineteenth century, Congress kept tight control of what administrative agencies were authorized to do. However, as Progressive ideas advanced and the executive branch was invested with more authority, concerns began to arise that the executive was receiving more authority than simply the power to execute the laws that Congress had enacted. The cases where this occurred reveal a pattern of increasing discretionary authority for executive branch agencies—all eventually approved by the Supreme Court—until the "great outline marked out by Congress" had completely disappeared. When that happened, in 1935 the Supreme Court finally acted to declare an unconstitutional delegation.

In 1892, for example, in *Field v. Clark*, the Supreme Court addressed a tariff case in which the statute was challenged as an unconstitutional delegation of legislative authority to the president. The statute had authorized the president to impose duties when he found certain facts pertaining to other countries' treatment of U.S. exports or imports into the United States. The Court, with Justice John Marshall Harlan delivering the opinion, found that the authority granted to the president was not legislative authority but merely the authority to carry out a legislative act:

Legislative power was exercised when Congress declared that the suspension should take effect upon a named contingency. What the President was required to do was simply in execution of the act of Congress. It was not the making of law. He was the mere agent of the lawmaking department to ascertain and declare the event upon which its expressed will was to take effect. It was a part of the law itself, as it left the hands of Congress, that the provisions, full and complete in themselves, permitting the free introduction of sugar, molasses, coffee, tea, and hides from particular countries should be suspended in a given contingency, and that in case of such suspension, certain duties should be imposed.

"The true distinction," as Judge Ranney, speaking for the Supreme Court of Ohio, has well said, "is between the delegation of power to make the law, which necessarily involves a *discretion as to what it shall be*, and conferring authority or discretion as to its execution, to be exercised under and in pursuance of the law. The first cannot be done; to the latter no valid objection can be made."[8]

This approach, in the first of a string of cases in which the Court examined whether there was an impermissible delegation to the executive, clearly follows Marshall's formulation. The important decision was made by Congress—that is, whether a consequence will follow upon the president's finding of a fact. The finding of the key fact is a purely administrative detail and does not involve a discretionary act.

The next case, *United States v. Grimaud,* was different. Ranchers indicted for grazing sheep on federal land challenged the constitutionality of the law that gave the secretary of agriculture broad authority to protect federal lands "against destruction by fire and depredation." There was no named contingency that required the secretary to make a finding as in *Field,* but the law authorized the secretary to act within a limited range: to prevent harm to the lands under his supervision. Within that limitation, the secretary was allowed considerable discretion to decide what rules to apply, and where, under his general authority. Administrative discretion, according to the Court, was thus confined by the general terms set by Congress:

[A] limited and regulated use for pasturage might not be inconsistent with the object sought to be attained by the statute. The determination of such questions, however, was a *matter of administrative detail.* What might be harmless in one forest might be harmful to another. What might be injurious at one stage of timber growth, or at one season of the year, might not be so at another.

In the nature of things, it was impracticable for Congress to provide general regulations for these various and varying details of management. Each reservation had its peculiar and special features, and, in authorizing the Secretary of Agriculture to meet these local conditions, Congress was merely conferring administrative functions upon an agent, and not delegating to him legislative power.[9]

Here, the Court simply decided that once the secretary had been provided with authority to protect federal lands from fire and depredation the decision about grazing was a matter of filling in the details, and did not rise to the level of a legislative decision. This followed the format used by Chief Justice Marshall in *Wayman*, where he decided that a delegation of authority to the judiciary, within a more general limitation established by Congress, was merely a detail.

In the 1928 case of *J. W. Hampton, Jr. v. United States*, another tariff case, the Supreme Court's nondelegation jurisprudence took a major turn away from the *Wayman* line. The president was authorized to increase a tariff rate in order to "equalize the...costs of production in the United States and the principal competing country." The law in question was close to what the Court had upheld in *Field v. Clark*, except that in this instance the president was given the power both to find that U.S. manufacturing interests were being injured and to adjust the tariffs to prevent the injury. This was substantially more discretion for the president than had been approved in *Field v. Clark*. In upholding the law against a claim that it was an unconstitutional delegation of authority, the Court adopted an entirely new theory, holding that, if Congress merely established an "intelligible principle" on which the president could act, that would be sufficient.

The Court's decision may have been influenced by the broad discretionary rate-making authority that, in 1887 and later, had been provided to the Interstate Commerce Commission but had never been challenged as unconstitutional; the Court may also have believed that it was necessary to provide a theory to support that delegation as well as the delegation in the tariff act under consideration. Accordingly, the Court addressed both:

> The same principle that permits Congress to exercise its ratemaking power in interstate commerce by declaring the rule which shall prevail in the legislative fixing of rates, and enables it to remit to a ratemaking body created in accordance with its provisions the fixing of such rates, justifies a similar provision for the fixing of customs duties on imported merchandise. If Congress shall lay down by legislative act an *intelligible principle* to which the person or body authorized to fix such rates is directed to conform, such legislative action is not a forbidden delegation of legislative power.[10]

Thus, both the "importance" and "great outline" ideas developed by Marshall were shunted aside in favor of a broader concept that was not well defined: an impermissible delegation would not be found if Congress provided an "intelligible principle" that the president or an administrative agency could follow. What exactly an intelligible principle was, and how it could be identified, was not made clear. Nevertheless, it was cited by the Supreme Court to approve delegations in several cases after *J. W. Hampton*,[11] and has allowed other courts, in later decisions, to categorize many items in legislation as intelligible principles and thus to avoid the difficult process of determining when legislative power had been unconstitutionally delegated.

Justice Thomas, the one current justice who has always taken the nondelegation doctrine seriously, has justifiably expressed doubt about the intelligible principle concept. Writing in yet another case where the intelligible principle was cited, he said: "I am not convinced that the intelligible principle doctrine serves to prevent all cessions of legislative power. I believe that there are cases in which the principle is intelligible and yet the significance of the delegated decision is simply too great for the decision to be called anything other than 'legislative.'"[12]

This brings us to the New Deal, and to the two cases where the Court actually did strike down what it believed were unconstitutional delegations of legislative authority.

The first of these was *Panama Refining v. Ryan*, in which an oil company challenged the president's order, as stated in section 9(c) of the National Industrial Recovery Act, to prohibit the interstate transportation of the firm's petroleum products. In an opinion written by Chief Justice Charles Evans Hughes, the Court began its analysis by pointing out the lack of standards in the power given to the president:

> Section 9(c) does not state whether or in what circumstances or under what conditions the President is to prohibit the transportation of the amount of petroleum or petroleum products produced in excess of the state's permission. It establishes no criteria to govern the President's course. It does not require any finding by the President as a condition of his action. The Congress...thus declares no *policy* as to the transportation of the excess production. So far as this section is concerned, it gives to the President an unlimited authority to determine the policy and to lay down the prohibition, or not to lay it down, as he may see fit. And disobedience to his order is made a crime punishable by fine and imprisonment.[13]

Then the Court concluded with this: "[F]rom the beginning of the government, the Congress has conferred upon executive officers the power to make regulations.... Such regulations become, indeed, binding rules of conduct, but they are valid only as subordinate rules and when found to be within the framework of the *policy* which the Legislature has sufficiently defined."[14]

This statement returned the analysis to Marshall's assessment in *Wayman*. The Court's theory here was that, in order to avoid an unconstitutional delegation of legislative authority, Congress had to set *some* standard that confined the president's (or any administrative agency's) discretion. But in this case the Court found that Congress had set no such standard, and thus had unconstitutionally delegated some of its legislative authority to the president.

The second case is the more famous *A.L.A. Schechter Poultry v. United States*, but it is actually of less interest from the standpoint of the nondelegation doctrine. In effect, the Court concluded that Congress, again without standards, had handed over legislative authority to private groups who would be able to establish rules of "fair competition." These rules would then be binding on their industry by operation of law after approval by the president. Again, in an opinion by Chief Justice Hughes, the Court struck down the underlying legislation, the National Industrial Recovery Act of 1933, as another unconstitutional delegation of legislative power:

> Section 3 of the Recovery Act is without precedent. It supplies no standards for any trade, industry or activity. It does not undertake to prescribe rules of conduct to be applied to particular states of fact determined by appropriate administrative procedure. Instead of prescribing rules of conduct, it authorizes the making of codes to prescribe them. *For that legislative undertaking, [section 3] sets up no standards,* aside from the statement of the general aims of rehabilitation, correction and expansion described in section one. In view of the scope of that broad declaration, and of the nature of the few restrictions that are imposed, *the discretion of the President in approving or prescribing codes, and thus enacting laws for the government of trade and industry throughout the country, is virtually unfettered.* We think that the code-making authority thus conferred is an unconstitutional delegation of legislative power.[15]

Although determining whether a delegation of legislative authority has occurred can be a difficult conceptual problem, there is no question that the Framers intended that the Judiciary make this determination. Here is Hamilton in *Federalist* No. 78, fully in accord with Marshall's views in both *Marbury* and *Wayman*:

> It is not…to be supposed, that the Constitution could intend to enable the representatives of the people to substitute their WILL to that of their constituents. It is far more rational to suppose, that the courts were designed to be an intermediate body between the people and the legislature, in order, among other things, *to keep the latter within the limits assigned to their authority.* The interpretation of the laws is the proper and peculiar province of the courts. A constitution is, in fact, and must be regarded by the judges, as a fundamental

law. It therefore belongs to them to ascertain its meaning, as well as the meaning of any particular act proceeding from the legislative body. (Emphasis added; in the Avalon edition, word in all caps is so in the original.)

Hamilton clearly recognized what treacherous territory this would be for the judiciary. As the only branch of the government that cannot claim some electoral support, the Supreme Court's action in striking down a law that was intended to combat a crisis, such as the Great Depression, would likely be unpopular with the public and expose the Court to retribution by Congress or the president. But this is exactly what Hamilton meant by "fortitude in the Judiciary"—the strength to stand up to the elected branches in support of the constitutional structure.

As usual, Hamilton was remarkably prescient. Shortly after his reelection with a massive congressional majority in 1936, President Roosevelt proposed that the number of members of the Supreme Court be expanded to sixteen, giving him the opportunity to appoint seven justices who would be more in sympathy with the New Deal. Because the Constitution does not specify the number of members of the Court, and the Congress was likely to be compliant, this was a very real threat to the independence of the judiciary, and one the Framers had not anticipated. Although public opposition, and a few obstinate Democratic committee chairs, ultimately defeated what was called the "court-packing plan," the Supreme Court seems to have recognized the gravity of the threat. On March 29, 1937, in two cases in which the chief justice wrote the majority opinions, the Court upheld two statutes that would previously have been constitutionally suspect. As former Chief Justice William Rehnquist described it:

In the case of *Jones & Laughlin v. NLRB*, which upheld the constitutionality of the Wagner Act, the Court markedly expanded upon its previous definitions of the scope of congressional authority to regulate commerce among the states. In *West Coast Hotel Company v. Parrish*, which upheld the state minimum-wage law, the Court all but abandoned its previous insistence that freedom of contract was protected by the Due Process Clause.[16]

In other words, the Court quickly backed away from challenging the constitutionality of commercial regulations and never again declared a law to be unconstitutional on the ground that it represented an unconstitutional delegation of legislative authority. The fact that the Supreme Court seems to have relinquished that role has had a profound effect on the courts' willingness and ability, since the New Deal, to control the growth of the administrative state. It also appears, along with *Chevron*, to have encouraged Congress to be even more open-handed with authority for administrative agencies, just at the time that it was ceding more political power and jurisdiction to the presidency.

How far the Court moved from *Panama Refining* and *Schechter* after 1937 is shown in *Yakus v. United States*, which involved the Emergency Price Control Act of 1942. There, the Court upheld a statute that granted the price administrator the authority to establish maximum prices for commodities throughout the United States. In this case, the Court upheld the statutory delegation because it found various standards in the authorizing statute that it considered sufficient to enable Congress, the public, and, presumably, the courts to determine whether "the will of Congress" was obeyed:

> The standards prescribed by the present Act, with the aid of the "statement of considerations" required to be made by the Administrator, are sufficiently definite and precise to enable Congress, the courts and the public to ascertain whether the Administrator, in fixing the designated prices, has conformed to those standards.... Hence we are unable to find in them an unauthorized delegation of legislative power.[17]

The dissent, by Justices Owen Roberts and Wiley Rutledge, however, found no such standards; they argued that the authority granted to the administrator was in fact an unconstitutional delegation of legislative authority:

Reflection will demonstrate that, in fact, the Act sets no limits upon the discretion or judgment of the Administrator. His commission is to take any action with respect to prices which he believes will preserve what he deems a sound economy during the emergency and prevent what he considers to be a disruption of such a sound economy in the postwar period. His judgment, founded, as it may be, on his studies and investigations, as well as other economic data, even though contrary to the great weight of current opinion or authority, is the final touchstone of the validity of his action.[18]

This case seemed to confirm that "legislation" was now not defined as what was "important" or "discretionary" but rather as an expression of some form of control over the administration of the law. As Cynthia R. Farina has written: "The administrative state became constitutionally tenable because the Court's vision of separation of powers evolved from the simple (but constraining) proposition that divided powers must not be commingled, to the more flexible (but far more complicated) proposition that power may be transferred *so long as* it will be adequately controlled."[19]

Although the Court never again struck down a law on grounds that it unconstitutionally delegated legislative authority, the dissent by Roberts and Rutledge in *Yakus* indicated that, at the least, the nondelegation doctrine was still alive. It was reintroduced in 1980 by Justice Rehnquist in *Industrial Union Department, AFL-CIO v. American Petroleum Institute*, known as the benzene case. While concurring in the majority's view to return a regulation to the Department of Labor, Rehnquist stated that he would have designated it as an unconstitutional delegation of legislative authority.

The issue in the case was a statute that required the secretary of labor to determine how much exposure to benzene—a hazardous material— was *feasible* (the key statutory word) to eliminate from the workplace. The Court was sharply divided, but Rehnquist's statement illustrates what a legislative decision actually is. "Read literally," Rehnquist wrote, "the relevant portion of [the statute] is completely precatory, admonishing the Secretary to adopt the most protective standard if he can, but excusing him from that duty if he cannot.... [T]he language of [the statute] gives the Secretary absolutely no indication where on the continuum of relative safety he should draw his line."[20] And, one might add, it sets no standard within which the discretion of the secretary could be exercised.

Rehnquist's point is correct. Members of Congress could not decide how much risk they wanted workers to bear; nor could they decide to force employers to find a substitute for benzene. So Congress avoided making a legislative decision—deciding between contending interests. Instead, as so often has occurred, Congress punted the decision to an administrative agency. "If Congress wishes to legislate in an area which it has not previously sought to enter," Rehnquist continued,

> it will, in today's political world, undoubtedly run into opposition no matter how the legislation is formulated. *But that is the very essence of legislative authority under our system.* It is the hard choices, and not the filling in of the blanks, which must be made by the elected representatives of the people. When fundamental policy decisions underlying important legislation about to be enacted are to be made, the buck stops with Congress and the President insofar as he exercises his constitutional role in the legislative process.[21]

With these ideas, it is difficult to imagine that, twenty years later, Chief Justice Rehnquist would agree with the Court's decision in *Whitman v. American Trucking Associations*, but he did. In that case, the goals-oriented Clean Air Act was challenged as an unconstitutional delegation of legislative authority. Writing for the Court, Justice Scalia described the principal element of the act as follows: "to set primary ambient air quality standards 'the attainment and maintenance of which...are requisite to protect the public health' with 'an adequate margin of safety.'"[22]

The decision reviewed virtually all the cases since *J. W. Hampton* and concluded that the Court had never found an unconstitutional delegation where Congress had laid down an "intelligible principle" for the agency to follow. What, then, was the intelligible principle in *Whitman*? It was the single word "requisite" in the statutory language, which the Court interpreted as "not lower or higher than is necessary...to protect the public health with an adequate margin of safety"; this, said the Court, "fits comfortably within the scope of discretion permitted by our precedent."[23] Unfortunately, given the widespread use of the meaningless intelligible principle idea, this was probably true.

After this 2001 decision, it became hard to imagine that there was anything of substance left of the important idea that Congress cannot delegate its legislative authority.

Legal Scholars and the Nondelegation Doctrine

Despite the Supreme Court's reluctance to enter the nondelegation thicket, some commentators and legal scholars continue to believe that the doctrine is necessary and viable. It is hard to disagree with this and still believe that the separation of powers and checks and balances in the Constitution have any long-term vitality.

Some scholars cite various ways that "legislative" action can be more easily identified. Martin Redish, for example, writes that legislative action involves "some meaningful level of *normative political commitment* by the enacting legislators, thus enabling the electorate to judge its representatives....Statutes that fail to make such a commitment, instead effectively amounting to nothing more than a mandate to an executive agency to create policy, should be deemed unconstitutional delegations of legislative power."[24] A "normative political commitment" is simply another way of saying a *legislative* decision—a difficult political decision that benefits some and disfavors others.

David Schoenbrod distinguishes between "goals statutes" and "rules statutes." The former merely state one or a series of goals but do not establish a policy by stepping on any toes; a rules statute, on the other hand, may have goals but makes the difficult arbitrary and discretionary decisions that constitute legislation:

> A rules statute requires the legislature to assume more responsibility
> and hence to be more accountable for the bearing of that respon-
> sibility than does a goals statute. In a rules statute, the legislature
> allocates rights and duties in the very course of indicating the kind
> of conduct that is permitted or not permitted. In a goals statute, the

legislature does not go that far; it indicates legislative hopes and requires a delegate to allocate rights and duties corresponding to those hopes. Given the political nature of the legislative process, a goals statute is likely to express popular hopes that are inherently contradictory and leave the delegate with the unhappy job of dealing with the people's disappointments and conflicts. In a goals statute, the legislature therefore tends to do only half a job—to distribute benefits without taking responsibility for the costs.[25]

A goals statute, then, does not reflect the important arbitrary and discretionary decisions that Congress must make in order to pursue its legislative responsibilities under the Constitution, and therefore an administrative agency must do the job that Congress was supposed to do. Accordingly, in this case, too, there are grounds for treating the underlying law as an unconstitutional delegation of legislative authority, because the administrative agency designated by Congress to meet the goals must then make the decisions that should have been made by Congress itself.

Ironically, while a goals statute, like the Clean Air Act of 1970, allows Congress to avoid controversy and take the credit for enacting a politically popular law, it does not make use of the unique power of Congress to set arbitrary requirements that cannot be challenged in the courts. As a result, while a goals statute can be more quickly enacted, it is likely to be less successful over time in reaching the policy objectives its sponsors desired. Thus if the courts were to force Congress to enact rules statutes—by more frequently striking down delegations of legislative authority—it is likely that there would be less litigation about rules and more effective and expeditious enforcement.

Unfortunately, since 1935 the courts have given a wide berth to economic regulation and have found a number of ways to avoid the difficult and controversial decision that a particular statute violates the nondelegation doctrine. As Gary Lawson has noted:

> The Supreme Court has resoundingly rejected every nondelegation challenge that it has considered since 1935, including challenges to statutes that instruct agencies to regulate based on the "public interest, convenience, or necessity" and to set "fair and equitable" prices.

After 1935, the Court has steadfastly maintained that Congress need only provide an "intelligible principle" to guide decisionmaking, and it has steadfastly found intelligible principles where less discerning readers find gibberish.[26]

This is true, if harsh, but Lawson—who supports the Marshall view in *Wayman* that the legislative decisions are the "important" decisions—nevertheless believes that Marshall's formulation is circular. After reviewing many other efforts to define a legislative act, he writes:

In essence, [all] the formulations examined... reduce to the proposition that Congress must make whatever decisions are sufficiently important to the relevant statutory scheme so that Congress must make them. In light of these prior efforts, I have elsewhere proposed as the appropriate nondelegation principle: 'Congress must make whatever policy decisions are sufficiently important to the statutory scheme at issue so that Congress must make them.' In other words, Chief Justice Marshall's circular formulation was right all along.[27]

I do not think this is quite correct. Although Marshall focused on decisions that are important when defining what is a legislative decision that must be made by Congress, he also said something else, which he seemed to equate with importance. Again, after noting that Congress could delegate an unimportant activity to the judicial branch, Marshall continued: "The power given to the Court to vary the mode of proceeding in this particular is a power to vary *minor regulations* which are *within the great outlines marked out by the legislature in directing the execution.*"[28] Here, Marshall is suggesting that "great outlines marked out by the legislature" are what validate the delegation of an unimportant authority to a subordinate agency. This is not circular. Marshall is saying that, once the legislature has defined the territory in which the subordinate agency can operate, its delegation of subordinate authority within that territory is constitutional.

It is difficult to find any specific set of principles among scholars who defend broad delegations of authority to administrative agencies.

There are few who contend that these open-handed delegations are *not* delegations of legislative authority; rather, they deem the issue not worth talking about, simply averring that administrative agencies are necessary, and leave it at that. A recent example is a 2017 article in the *Harvard Law Review* by Gillian E. Metzger, in which she writes: "By refusing to recognize the administrative state's essential place in our constitutional order, contemporary anti-administrativism forestalls development of a separation of powers analysis better tailored to the reality of current government."[29] This is followed by: "Many government programs are popular or lobbied for by well-connected interest groups....Presidents need the administrative state to achieve their policy goals....Enactment of burdensome procedural constraints or legislation retracting deference would only serve to make the Trump Administration's efforts to repeal regulations significantly harder."[30]

In other words, according to Metzger, the constitutional structure must yield to the reality that the administrative state is here to stay, and rather than worry about what the Framers had in mind for protecting liberty, or the checks and balances system, it would be more sensible to find a way to fit the agencies of the administrative state into today's legal reality than attempt to overturn it. After all, even the Trump administration will benefit from the continued growth in the power of the administrative state. It is hard to call this true legal analysis, let alone a serious treatment of the Constitution, but it reflects the dismissive attitude of some—first seen in the Progressive movement—toward major constitutional issues.

Finally, while the administrative state has widespread support among legal scholars, there is very little concern about where it gets its legitimacy. Why should these administrative agencies be able to command obedience to their rules? This question was put to Adrian Vermeule of Harvard Law School, one of the most prolific writers on administrative law, in a 2016 Cato Institute written scholarly debate under the title "Questioning the Administrative State." In this exchange of views, Vermeule delivered an essay titled "What Legitimacy Crisis?" Although he lays out his views on why the legitimacy of administrative agencies is beyond question, his essay turns out to be a clear demonstration of the reasons why we should all be concerned.

First, he addresses the question whether Congress has in fact been delegating its legislative powers to administrative agencies.

> It has never been the theory of American law that Congress gives away legislative power whenever it grants statutory authority to agencies, although if the grant is excessively broad or vague, and thus lacks an "intelligible principle" to guide administrative discretion, a genuine problem of unconstitutional delegation may arise. In the normal case, agencies acting within the boundaries of their statutory authority exercise executive power, not legislative power.[31]

This seems to assume the issue, which is whether the agencies of the administrative state are in fact *always*—not just in the normal case—"acting within the boundaries of their statutory authority." Chapter 1, on the rule of law, offers many examples that question this premise, and of course the goals-oriented environmental laws on clean air and water are additional examples of goals statutes that contain few if any boundaries.

Vermeule further contends that

> *arguments in praise of Congress and classical lawmaking are themselves arguments in praise of the administrative state.* It is not as though the administrative state was created against Congress's wishes. . . . Whatever legitimacy Congress possesses transfers to the agencies. If we think that Congress possesses unique deliberative capacities, or uniquely representative properties, we should also think that Congress will delegate when it makes good sense to do so, after well-conducted deliberation and in an appropriately representative way.[32]

However, in chapter 3, we saw that Congress has incentives *not* to make the difficult decisions that legislation requires, and that this is encouraged when the courts allow agencies wide discretion in interpreting their legislative authority.

Vermeule then asserts that "very few or no statutory delegations are blank checks. . . . Congress almost always delegates under substantive and procedural constraints, expanding or contracting agency authority incrementally."[33] One can imagine that Congress "almost always" imposes restrictions on administrative agencies; but the very words imply that there are times when it does not, and there are also times when the agencies expand on what authority they have been given, even when accompanied by constraints on their discretion. The issue is how often this occurs and what to do about it. As shown in this book, it occurs often enough to be of concern on the question of legitimacy, and the reason it occurs is that the courts—through deference and otherwise—allow and encourage it to occur.

Finally, Vermeule argues that "an independently elected President is one of the great constitutional checks on the bureaucracy. By shaping and constraining the behavior of the administrative state, the President contributes to and helps to ensure its legitimacy, transferring to it his own legitimacy as the sole elected official with a colorable claim to represent the nation as a whole."[34] This statement may refer to an assumed political value of a connection to the president, but even as that it is fanciful. The president has little or no effect on "shaping and constraining" the more than three thousand regulations that are issued every year by agencies of the administrative state. Nor does the president have a constitutional role in legitimizing these regulations; if they are legislative in nature, they must be made by Congress, and if they are subordinate—filling in the details—they are valid when made by the agencies acting within the authority of a statute. The president himself would be acting illegitimately if his action was not authorized by the Constitution or by congressional enactment. He cannot then legitimize regulations that are not themselves consistent with the Constitution or statute law.

To claim that the president's election legitimates all the rules and regulations made by administrative agencies during his presidency is simply to evade an issue by ignoring reality. Reality, indeed, was demonstrated in 2017, when the Trump administration sought to cut back the issuance of regulations by federal agencies and made only limited inroads. If Vermeule and others were correct in believing that the president is a "constitutional check" on rulemaking, the Trump administration would have been more successful than it was in 2017. But they are not correct; what they rely on as a source of administrative legitimacy is a myth. Regrettably, Vermeule's arguments in support of the administrative state show only how serious the legitimacy problem is.

Under the Constitution, legitimacy does not come solely from being elected. It is clear that the judiciary, though unelected, has legitimacy to declare legislation unconstitutional or otherwise to overthrow administrative rules. The judiciary's legitimacy comes from its constitutional role as recited in Article III, and from its role in the constitutional structure as described by the Framers generally, by Alexander Hamilton in *Federalist No. 78*, and by Chief Justice Marshall in *Marbury v. Madison*. In addition, as recently as 1946, with the enactment of the Administrative Procedure Act, Congress specifically authorized judicial review of administrative rules. The Senate judiciary committee report on the bill contained the following language: "Judicial review is of utmost importance.... It is indispensable since its mere existence generally precludes the arbitrary exercise of powers or the assumption of powers not granted."[35]

Fortunately, as discussed in the next chapter, recent developments on the Supreme Court in relation to *Chevron* offer some hope that the Court is refocusing on the responsibilities of the judiciary under the constitutional structure. If so, the nondelegation doctrine could come back to life.

Stirrings at the Supreme Court

The failure of the Supreme Court—most recently in *Whitman v. American Trucking Associations*—to challenge congressional legislation that hands open-ended legislative authority to the agencies of the administrative state, is a serious failure to carry out the responsibilities that the judiciary was supposed to perform under the Constitution. It is also the most important single reason that the administrative state has continued to grow out of control. If there is no longer a court-enforced nondelegation doctrine, then Congress can authorize agencies to prescribe "such rules and regulations as may be necessary or appropriate for the public's interest or convenience" and go home to campaign for reelection.

Congress has written many laws this way, and they have been confirmed by the Supreme Court. In *National Broadcasting Co. v. United States*,[36] for example, the Court upheld the FCC's power to regulate broadcasting "in the public interest." This is certainly acceptable to Congress, since it often adopts "goals" statutes that avoid controversy by simply handing the difficult issues to a regulatory agency. In these cases, both the Supreme Court and Congress have defaulted in their respective responsibilities under the Constitution to adopt real legislation (in the case of Congress), or to protect the constitutional structure (in the case of the courts).

Just as some scholarly commentators refuse to accept that the nondelegation doctrine is dead, there are some indications of restlessness on the Supreme Court itself. In *Whitman*, the majority opinion upheld an EPA regulation against a nondelegation challenge to the Clean Air Act. There were many concurring opinions, suggesting that the Court was not united on the reasoning but believed that Congress had provided an "intelligible principle," as weak as that seemed when described in the majority opinion. Although Justice Thomas concurred in the result, he questioned the efficacy of the intelligible principle concept and remarked: "On a future day...I would be willing to address the question whether our delegation jurisprudence has strayed too far from our Founders' understanding of separation of powers."[37]

This was the first indication that a sitting justice would be willing to revisit the underpinning of the nondelegation doctrine. Another opportunity came in 2015, with the Court's decision in *Department of Transportation v. Association of American Railroads*, in which Justice Thomas wrote a much longer concurrence that ended with this:

> We have too long abrogated our duty to enforce the separation of powers required by our Constitution. We have overseen and sanctioned the growth of an administrative system that concentrates the power to make laws and the power to enforce them in the hands of a vast and unaccountable administrative apparatus that finds no comfortable home in our constitutional structure. The end result may be trains that run on time (although I doubt it), but the cost is to our Constitution and the individual liberty it protects.[38]

This may not be the last word, and Justice Thomas may not be alone in his concerns. The quote from Chief Justice Roberts that heads this chapter suggests that he and Justice Alito, who joined him in dissent, are aware of the Court's responsibility to keep the other branches within their assigned lanes. Justice Gorsuch has not yet expressed a view, but as an appellate judge he dissented in a 2015 criminal case in which a statute provided extraordinary discretionary authority to the attorney general to deal with sex offenders. His dissent made clear that he would not accept an "intelligible principle" as a sufficient standard in a criminal case. Whether his concerns extend to noncriminal cases is yet to be determined, but much of the analysis in this long dissent would be equally applicable outside a criminal context.[39]

If Judge Kavanaugh is confirmed, he would be the fifth justice to show strong support for the separation of powers by requiring Congress to set the standards for administrative agencies. This is often seen as a challenge to *Chevron*, and it certainly is, but it is also an endorsement of the nondelegation doctrine. In a 2017 case involving the FCC's net neutrality rule (which was upheld by the Court of Appeals for the D.C. Circuit) Kavanaugh dissented from a denial of a rehearing, arguing that, "If an agency wants to exercise expansive regulatory authority over some major social or economic activity . . . an *ambiguous* grant of statutory authority is not enough. Congress must clearly authorize an agency to take a major regulatory action."[40]

Until then, the nondelegation doctrine remains in limbo. The Constitution still requires a separation of powers, and in the constitutional structure Congress is still supposed to wield the legislative power. But the courts have not been able, after more than two hundred years, to develop a definition of "legislation" that will enable them to carry out what the Framers expected them to do. Instead, they have settled for an "intelligible principle" to paper over the problem and justify their failure to hold Congress to account.

As outlined in chapter 3, there are many reasons why Congress does not want to engage in the heavy lifting involved in true legislative work, so we can expect goals-oriented legislation to continue to challenge the Supreme Court. The Court cannot formally abandon the nondelegation doctrine, but it will not be able to prevent continuing challenges as long as it allows Congress to avoid its own constitutional responsibilities.

7

THE *CHEVRON* DOCTRINE

*For I agree, that "there is no liberty, if the power of judging be not
separated from the legislative and executive powers."... Liberty can have
nothing to fear from the judiciary alone, but would have everything to
fear from its union with either of the other departments.*

ALEXANDER HAMILTON, *FEDERALIST* No. 78,
QUOTING MONTESQUIEU

*Judicial review is of utmost importance.... It is indispensable since its
mere existence generally precludes the arbitrary exercise of powers or the
assumption of powers not granted.*

SENATE REPORT ON THE ADMINISTRATIVE PROCEDURE ACT

Whether the courts support or reject the nondelegation doctrine is not the only issue that determines whether the administrative state will continue to grow. A unanimous decision of the Supreme Court in 1984, *Chevron v. Natural Resources Defense Council,* might be better described as the "easy delegation doctrine," because it has provided a foundation for administrative agencies to expand the scope of their authority beyond the language that Congress actually enacted, without Congress specifically delegating what might be considered legislative authority.

The case arose under the Clean Air Act, which required a "major stationary source" of air pollution to seek a permit for any new equipment that would increase the volume of its emissions. The statute did not define "major stationary source," and the EPA later concluded that it could be an entire contiguous industrial facility (which the Court called the "bubble" concept) owned by the same company. This would permit a firm like Chevron to avoid seeking a permit for new equipment that would increase its emissions if the firm reduced its emissions somewhere else in the same bubble. This new interpretation was opposed by the Natural Resources Defense Council, and while the NRDC lost this battle, the advocacy group—and all those who want administrative agencies to have more power—definitely won the war.

In an opinion written by Justice John Paul Stevens, the Court approved the EPA's new interpretation, outlining a two-step process for determining the validity of the decision the agency had made. First, said the Court, if the statute was clear about what Congress wanted, that was the end of the matter. However, "if the statute is silent or ambiguous with respect to the specific issue, the question for the court is whether the agency's answer is based on a permissible construction of the statute."[1] Up to this point, it would still make sense for a court—through traditional judicial review—to construe whether the agency presented a "permissible construction of the statute."

But the Court then went a step further: "Sometimes the legislative delegation to an agency on a particular question is implicit, rather than explicit. In such a case, a court may not substitute its own construction of a statutory provision for a reasonable interpretation made by the administrator of an agency."[2] This idea—that courts may not substitute their own judgment for a "reasonable interpretation" by the agency—when applied to "delegations" that are both explicit and "implicit"—has become known as *Chevron* deference. What it seems to mean is that administrative agencies may infer powers that Congress has not explicitly granted as long as that inference is "reasonable."

It is easy to see what a major change this worked in the relationship between courts and administrative agencies. When the nondelegation doctrine was in force, the courts could (though they usually did not) exert some discipline over the tendencies of Congress to avoid controversy by passing major decisions to administrative agencies. As long as that doctrine had not been formally abandoned, it was still within the province of the courts to say "what the law is," as Chief Justice Marshall phrased it in *Marbury*. This would require that the courts apply to agency interpretations of statutory language the kind of textual analysis that at least gave the courts the final say about what Congress meant.

The *Chevron* Difference Is *Chevron* Deference

But under *Chevron*, in cases where the statutory language did not specifically authorize or prohibit an administrative decision under review, lower courts were directed to defer to the agency's interpretation of its statutory authority if that interpretation was "reasonable." Certainly, this still gave the courts an opening to find an agency's interpretation "unreasonable," but it was a narrow cleft. If we look further at the language of *Chevron*, and how it has been enforced by the Supreme Court, we can see how narrow this actually was.

The Court's reasoning process was extraordinary, considering that the decision was unanimous. First, quoting an earlier case, the Court noted that if the agency's "'choice represents a reasonable accommodation of conflicting policies that were committed to the agency's care by the statute, we should not disturb it unless it appears from the statute or its legislative history that the accommodation is not one that Congress would have sanctioned.'"[3] So lower courts were told that the burden of proof, so to speak, was on them to show that Congress would not have agreed with what the agency did. Then the Court turned to the actual decision of the D.C. Circuit Court of Appeals in *Chevron* and found that it had "misconceived the nature of its role in reviewing the regulations at issue. Once it determined, after its own examination of the legislation, that Congress did not actually have an intent regarding the applicability of the bubble concept to the permit program, the question before it was...whether the Administrator's view...[was] a reasonable one."[4]

After reviewing the legislative history of the Clean Air Act and determining that Congress had never considered the issue of whether a stationary source was a single building or a group of facilities under common ownership, the Court turned to what it called "policy." "[T]he Administrator's interpretation," said the Court, "represents a reasonable accommodation of manifestly competing interests, and is entitled to deference:...the agency considered the matter in a detailed and reasoned fashion, and the decision involves reconciling conflicting policies. Congress intended to accommodate both interests, but did not do so itself on the level of specificity presented by these cases."[5]

Finally, and remarkably, the Court continued with this:

> [P]erhaps Congress was unable to forge a coalition on either side of the question, and those on each side decided to take their chances with the scheme devised by the agency. For judicial purposes, it matters not [exactly how this occurred].... While agencies are not directly accountable to the people, the Chief Executive is, and it is entirely appropriate for this political branch of the Government to make such policy choices—resolving the competing interests which Congress itself either inadvertently did not resolve, or intentionally left to be resolved by the agency charged with the administration of the statute in light of everyday realities.[6]

There are several important things to note about this language. First, it substantially downgrades the role of Congress in deciding questions of national policy. In the Court's view, if Congress cannot decide how to resolve competing interests, administrative agencies can do it instead, and this apparently applies to issues that were either too difficult for Congress to resolve, or that Congress "implicitly" (but nevertheless deliberately) left for the agency to resolve. In addition, on the all-important question of where the agency gets the authority to decide these matters—after all, Congress has clearly not decided them—the Court is silent. To the extent that it addresses the matter, the Court assumes that the agency's authority comes from its connection, through the executive branch, to an elected president who is ultimately accountable to the people. The Court seems to assume that the president made the decision to adopt the "bubble" idea and passed it down to the EPA, and while that might have been true in this particular case it is most certainly untrue for the thousands of other rules that are issued by administrative agencies each year. Nevertheless, the decision was written, and has certainly been applied by the lower courts, on the basis of the fiction that every decision by an administrative agency is a consequence of a presidential or administration policy.

Ultimately, then, the Court required deference to *any* administrative decision that a court deems "reasonable," without regard to whether it might usurp the power of Congress. One does not have to think very deeply about this concept before seeing it as a virtual nullification of the separation of powers. The legislative power of Congress—transferred to an administrative agency because it is part of the executive branch—is now combined with the executive authority that the Constitution confers on the president. Madison would have been appalled.

After reading these passages in *Chevron*, one might well wonder what role Congress now had in making law. The Court called the decision one of "policy" and noted that Congress did not reconcile either the "conflicting interests" or the "conflicting policies" that arose out of them, suggesting at the same time that Congress could have decided to leave the reconciliation of these conflicts for resolution by the administrative agency. If administrative agencies are now supposed to have this role, Congress becomes merely a benevolent source of legislative power for administrative agencies, not a legislative body that itself resolves major issues for the country.

The whole purpose of a legislature is to reconcile the conflicting interests and the conflicting policies they produce. That's why the decisions of a legislature can be arbitrary and wholly discretionary, unreviewable except to the extent that they violate the Constitution. Now, under *Chevron*, the entity that reconciles the conflicting interests in U.S. society is to be an administrative agency—a group of bureaucrats living in the Washington, D.C., area, who in no way represent the people who actually have those conflicting interests.

We have encountered this concept before, in the chapter on the Progressive Era, where the Progressive idea was that expert, educated, scientifically knowledgeable, credentialed, and disinterested public servants would make the important decisions for the American people—after, of course, becoming imbued with the correct sense of the public's will. That Progressive impulse, which had been preserved through the New Deal, showed up once again in *Chevron*. The Court was not bothered by the idea that the federal bureaucracies in Washington would make the decisions that Congress itself would not or could not make. What appears to have been important to the *Chevron* Court was not who—among the

Congress, the agencies, or the president—actually made the decisions for the American people as long as it was not the judiciary:

> When a challenge to an agency construction of a statutory provision, fairly conceptualized, really centers on the wisdom of the agency's policy, rather than whether it is a reasonable choice within a gap left open by Congress, the challenge must fail. In such a case, federal judges—who have no constituency—have a duty to respect legitimate policy choices made by those who do. The responsibilities for assessing the wisdom of such policy choices and resolving the struggle between competing views of the public interest are not judicial ones: "Our Constitution vests such responsibilities in the political branches."[7]

While this formulation was generally correct about the role of the judiciary in a policy context, it was a question never in doubt and thus a ringing statement of the obvious. The Framers expected the judiciary, and particularly the Supreme Court, to protect a constitutional structure in which the legislature and the executive were intended to be performing separate functions. The real issue for the Court in *Chevron*, accordingly, was not to warn the judiciary away from policy making—that was a given—but ultimately to decide *which* of the elected branches should have made the decision that was presented to the Court. To go back to Chief Justice Marshall's formulation, if the decision was important, it should have been made by Congress; if not, it could be made by the executive branch within the area outlined by Congress.

However, the Court assumed this central question away, by declaring that an administrative agency—as opposed to a court—was the proper venue for a policy decision because of the agency's connection, through the executive branch, to an elected president. This is entirely unsatisfactory. Under any reading of the Constitution, an administrative agency is the correct locus for a decision only on those policy questions that are not important enough to be made by Congress, and even then only where the agency has been authorized by Congress to make the decision. In *Chevron*, however, the Court never considered this key element of the separation of powers. Instead, it directed lower courts to defer to administrative agencies in *every case* where Congress had not spoken clearly and the administrative agency's decision was "reasonable." This cannot be correct. There must be some cases—at least in constitutional theory—where an administrative agency has made a rule on a matter that exceeds the authority it was given by Congress, but the *Chevron* Court seemed to believe that the only relevant question is whether the decision has been made by one of the elected branches—and assumes that a decision by an executive branch agency under all circumstances is entitled to the same respect as a decision by Congress.

The decision was wrong for two additional reasons. First, in basing its decision on the notion that an administrative agency is the correct locus for policy decisions because of its connection to the president—an accountable elected official—the Court implicitly invoked the fictional idea that the president somehow directs agencies of the executive branch to issue the more than twelve thousand rules and regulations that will be issued during the president's four-year term. As noted in earlier chapters, only a tiny few "major rules" are even brought to the attention of OMB (which is at least within the Executive Office of the President), and fewer still are rules that might ever be brought to the president's attention. It is true that in a legal and political sense all the members of the executive branch are subject to some degree of control by the president, and that is certainly true for those the president appoints to, and can remove from, an office within his administration. But unless the president has spoken on a particular issue, the members of the vast federal bureaucracy—protected against dismissal by Civil Service rules—simply continue with the process of issuing rules and regulations based on laws that were enacted before the current president took office. There is no better evidence of this than the fact that, while President Trump made the reduction in regulations a key element of his economic policy, the actual reduction during 2017 was relatively small—and the total still exceeded three thousand, as it has in every year since 1993. This demonstrates that, in the rulemaking process, the administrative state is largely unaffected by, and for the most part uninterested in, whatever it is that the president wants.

Indeed, some presidents have joked about their lack of power over the bureaucracy. President Truman said of his successor: "He'll sit here, and he'll say, 'Do this! Do that!' And nothing will happen. Poor Ike—it won't be a bit like the Army." President Kennedy is said to have remarked that dealing with the bureaucracy "is like trying to nail jelly to the wall," and, in reply to an interlocutor, "I agree with you, but I don't know if the government will."

Yes, for the occasional and rare issue on which the president wants to establish a particular policy, he can force that policy to prevail if he works at it; but for the more than three thousand regulations that are issued every year, the president likely had no idea that they were issued in his name or by his administration.

The second reason *Chevron* was wrong is that, if the Court's decision can in any way be fit into a separation of powers framework, it is by assuming that the EPA's decision on the meaning of "stationary source" was not an "important decision," in Chief Justice Marshall's terms. In that case, it would be fully appropriate for an administrative agency to make the decision that the EPA made in this instance. As a matter of fact, despite the challenge to the decision by the NRDC, whether a stationary source was one building or many under common ownership could easily be seen as an unimportant decision, just a filling in of the details in a major piece of legislation, and that would explain why Congress did not deal with it.

If the Court had taken that position, its view would then have informed all later cases in which the question was whether a particular administrative decision was important or unimportant, much like the evolving law on search and seizure or interstate commerce. This would have followed up on and added texture to the Marshall idea that Congress makes the important decisions and the administrative agencies make the unimportant ones.

Instead, the Court avoided making this simple decision by developing an elaborate structure that allowed agencies to resolve issues that Congress hadn't even considered, authorizing them to do so—and to receive deference—when a court decides that what the agency has done is "reasonable." In adopting this position, the Court permitted administrative agencies to take on the role of Congress in the Framers' structure, and, by divesting courts of the authority to determine through judicial review which powers Congress had actually granted to administrative agencies, the Court significantly empowered the administrative state.

Moreover, the Court did not seem to realize that by telling lower courts to evaluate whether an agency's decision was "reasonable" it was thrusting the courts into exactly the kind of judgment about policy that it said they should avoid. If what the Court meant in *Chevron* was that an agency's decision was "reasonable" within the scope of the legislative language that Congress had enacted, that could have been read as an endorsement of traditional judicial review. But throughout its opinion the Court associates the term "reasonable" with the term "policy"—as in "the EPA's use of [the bubble concept] here is a reasonable policy choice for the agency to make"[8]—leaving lower courts in the position of having to decide whether an administrative ruling was reasonable in a policy sense, not simply as an interpretation of the relevant statute. As outlined in chapter 1, it is tempting—but wrong from the standpoint of the rule of law—for courts to decide what Congress meant as a matter of policy rather than what Congress actually enacted.

On another level, there is a sense in which a judge deferring to an administrative agency's interpretation of a statute is giving up his or her independent role as a judge and subordinating the law to administrative ukase. Philip Hamburger writes:

> When deferring to administrative lawmaking, interpretation, and factfinding, judges must consider whether, instead of exercising independent judgment about the law, they are bowing to a power above the law. This was the theory on which absolute monarchs expected judges to defer to prerogative power, and when judges now defer to such power in administrative form, they evidently are again submitting to a power above the law.[9]

To be clear, whether the courts should review administrative fact-finding, as Hamburger suggests, is not a matter under consideration here. This book is concerned solely with whether administrative agencies have, or should have—in the rulemaking process—the power to determine the scope of their statutory powers. On that, too, Hamburger's point is applicable.

Finally, there is another *Chevron* element that deserves attention—the question whether *Chevron* has forced the courts to accept the administrative agency's interpretation of the law rather than the interpretation of an adverse litigant. This is not a question of statutory interpretation; it is a question of fairness, due process, and the rule of law. As Hamburger pointed out in a 2017 op-ed: "Where the government is a party to a case, *Chevron* requires judges to defer to the agency's interpretation. This amounts to a precommitment to the government's legal position. *Chevron,* in other words, forces judges to engage in systematic bias favoring one party—the most powerful of parties—in violation of the Fifth Amendment's due process of law."[10]

Because of its acceptance of the idea that courts should defer to administrative positions under almost all circumstances, the Framers would have seen the *Chevron* decision as a threat to the separation of powers and thus as a threat to liberty. They were aware of the possibility that the legislature and the executive could under certain circumstances combine their forces, posing a threat to liberty, but in this event they relied on the judiciary to step in—as it did most recently in the Choke Point case discussed in chapter 1. *Chevron* would have been seen as the judiciary's failing to meet its constitutional responsibilities. As Hamilton wrote in *Federalist* No. 78, "Liberty can have nothing to fear from the judiciary alone, but would have everything to fear from its union with either of the other departments." In a sense, through *Chevron*, the judiciary has thrown in its lot with the executive branch.

Hamilton also argues in *Federalist* No. 78 that the judiciary should have life tenure: "as nothing can contribute so much to its firmness and independence as permanency in office, this quality may therefore be justly regarded as an indispensable ingredient in its constitution, and, in a great measure, as the citadel of the public justice and the public security." In other words, the judiciary was given life tenure so as to enable it to stand up to the elected branches. But in *Chevron* the Supreme Court turns this idea on its head by saying that the judiciary should defer to administrative agencies' decisions as to what a statute means, precisely because these agencies are part of an elected branch.

Judicial Restraint and Judicial Activism

In the Framers' design, the judiciary has two distinct roles, as interpreters of the Constitution's language and as defenders of the Constitution's structure—or, as Hamilton put it, as "the guardians of the Constitution." When the courts consider the constitutionality of statutes that implicate the substantive language of the Constitution, judicial restraint might certainly be called for; it is reasonable to assume, in these cases, that Congress should be given extensive latitude, within the Constitution's language, to work its will through legislation.

Arguments for judicial restraint are not as compelling, however, when it is the constitutional *structure* that is under consideration. The Framers specifically delegated the preservation of that structure to the judiciary, and it should be preserved until changed through the mechanisms the Constitution itself established. In other words, laws and policies deserve to be respected because the Framers assumed that any changes in the laws would be the province of Congress. They did not see the Supreme Court as having any authority to change the constitutional structure. Indeed, it has an affirmative obligation to guard and preserve that structure.

The Framers designed a carefully balanced government system, which they thought was essential for the preservation of liberty. In this system, each of the three branches had a specific role and the ability to check the other two. The judiciary's role was to prevent either of the elected branches from overstepping its constitutional bounds, and to carry out that role—as Hamilton's statements in *Federalist* No. 78 make clear—the judiciary was given the benefit of lifetime appointment so that the courts could stand up to the much more powerful political branches.

As discussed in the previous chapter, since FDR's court-packing plan in 1937, the judiciary has not used its inherent power to declare that a statute has unconstitutionally delegated legislative authority to the executive. If the Supreme Court has in fact permanently given up this authority—or, as in *Whitman v. American Trucking Associations*, will not treat it seriously—the Framers' system falls apart. Congress would then be able to enact legislation that simply sets goals, while transferring to administrative agencies the power to address the difficult societal problems that a legislature is supposed to resolve. If this occurs, there is no point in judicial review of laws passed by Congress. Goals legislation contains nothing to review.

Such a dismal scenario might be attractive to Congress, allowing its members to get political credit for setting goals but not requiring them to do the heavy lifting that real legislation involves. It might also be acceptable to Congress when the same political party controls both chambers and the presidency, a subject discussed in chapter 4. Assuming, however, that the nondelegation doctrine is not dead, as some claim, and that the Supreme Court will invoke it in appropriate circumstances, *Chevron* deference becomes an important avenue through which to avoid a finding that Congress has unconstitutionally delegated its legislative authority. In *Chevron,* the Court seemed to surrender its power to interpret whether a particular rule or regulation went beyond the authority conferred by Congress.

The underlying reasons for this, especially since the decision was unanimous, are unclear. Although they came from different legal traditions, each of the six justices who participated in the consideration of the case found reasons to concur. Certainly, some of the ideas that were born in the Progressive Era continue to be influential with jurists whose worldview comes from that background. There is a tendency among today's Progressives to see administrative agencies as benign, and operated—as the earlier Progressives saw it—by educated, public-spirited people who have the best interests of the American people in view. For the conservatives on the Court, as well as those who believe in the primacy of a democratic political system, the objective of reducing the role of the courts in the policy process might have been paramount in their decision. These ideas are at the root of the conservative view that the courts under all circumstances should exercise judicial restraint, and to interfere as little as possible in the decision-making process of the elected branches. Justice Scalia, for example, one of the strongest supporters of *Chevron*, was also a powerful advocate for judicial restraint and an opponent of what was called judicial activism.

It may be that the issues of judicial activism and judicial restraint have gained adherents among judges and justices because of severe criticism of the Court's social policy decisions over the last fifty years. But it is important to recognize that these decisions were based on the Court's interpretations of the Constitution's words, not its role in preserving the Constitution's structure. The Framers would never have imagined that the Supreme Court, on questions of the proper role of Congress or the executive in the constitutional structure, would conclude that its position should be one of judicial restraint. The executive was to carry out the laws that Congress passed, and the judiciary was to interpret whether both Congress and the executive were doing this properly. Whether or not these two branches are elected is wholly irrelevant. The Framers' theory was that the people, in the belief that the separation of powers it embodied would preserve liberty, had adopted the supreme law—the Constitution— and the judiciary was bound to enforce it, irrespective of whether the branch involved was or was not elected by the people. On these principles, there should be no judicial restraint. *Chevron*, however, suggests that the Supreme Court has lost sight of this responsibility.

Thus, where the Court believes that Congress has delegated an impermissible portion of its legislative authority to an administrative agency or to the president, it should not hesitate to invoke the nondelegation doctrine. The Constitution itself provides ways for the people to change it, but until that happens the judiciary is bound to serve as the guardian of the Constitution's structure; there really is no alternative. If Congress is willing to hand its powers over to the executive, the judiciary has an obligation to step in. But the outcome is no different if—as in *Chevron*—the Supreme Court directs lower courts to defer to the decisions of administrative agencies about the scope of their statutory authorities. In both cases the role of Congress as the exclusive source of legislation for the government has been compromised, and liberty is threatened. The fact that this occurred through an agency's arrogation of power instead of a direct delegation by Congress should make no difference.

Where an agency has assumed powers it was not granted by Congress, the courts have more latitude, including the possible remedies described below, but the issue is the same; Congress, under the Framers' plan, was to make the laws, and the courts were to interpret their meaning. Agencies going beyond what Congress actually enacted cannot be permissible—in that case the agencies involved are engaged in legislating—and judicial restraint on this subject is a derogation of the role of the judiciary in the constitutional structure.

A Crack in the *Chevron* Wall?

The judiciary's deference to administrative agencies did not begin with *Chevron*; it was already present in Supreme Court jurisprudence as early as 1945, with a Supreme Court decision in *Bowles v. Seminole Rock*. In that case, the wartime price-control agency had reinterpreted its rules on the maximum allowable price of crushed rock. Challenged by a crushed rock producer, the change was upheld by the Court, noting that the decision of the price administrator—which was a new interpretation of his own rule—"has controlling weight unless it is plainly erroneous or inconsistent with the regulation."[11] Later, the deference principle announced there became known as *Auer* deference when it was restated for a unanimous Court by Justice Scalia in a 1997 case, *Auer v. Robbins*. "Because the [interpretation at issue] is a creature of the Secretary's own regulations," Justice Scalia wrote, "his interpretation of it is, under our jurisprudence, controlling unless 'plainly erroneous or inconsistent with the regulation.'"[12] In this light, *Chevron* can be seen as just a continuation of the gradual deterioration of the judiciary's role in challenging administrative authority that began in the Progressive Era.

However, in 2013 the formerly solid Supreme Court view on *Chevron* began to split, suggesting that a new interpretation and downgrading of the case may be in the offing. The case before the Court was *City of Arlington v. FCC*, and involved the authority of the FCC to set a "reasonable period of time" during which a locality must make a siting decision on wireless facilities. Two Texas cities argued that the FCC did not have the authority to interpret the term under the applicable statute. The majority opinion of the Court, upholding the FCC's position, was written by Justice Scalia, but Chief Justice Roberts wrote a dissent in which Justices Kennedy and Alito joined.

As background, it is important to understand that Justice Scalia was one of the Court's strongest supporters of *Chevron*, and in this case—facing a strong dissent from his usual Court allies—he pulled out all the stops (even for Scalia), claiming that the dissenters were making a false distinction between the jurisdiction of an agency and its decisions on policy. There was in fact no way, he argued, to distinguish between these two elements of administrative law, and thus *Chevron* applies to both. As a matter of legal policy, he noted, *Chevron* should not be challenged because it "provides a stable background rule against which Congress can legislate: Statutory ambiguities will be resolved, within the bounds of reasonable interpretation, not by the courts but by the administering agency."[13] Further: "The [idea that there should be a distinction between jurisdiction and policy] is an empty distraction because every new application of a broad statutory term can be reframed as a questionable extension of the agency's jurisdiction."[14] Further still: "The false dichotomy between 'jurisdictional' and 'non-jurisdictional' agency interpretations may be no more than a bogeyman, but it is dangerous all the same. Like the Hound of the Baskervilles, it is conjured by those with a greater quarry in sight: Make no mistake—the ultimate target here is *Chevron* itself."[15]

Scalia was wrong about the jurisdictional/nonjurisdictional dichotomy—that was not the point of Roberts's dissent—but he was correct that the dissent was proposing a new and weaker version of *Chevron* that, if adopted by the Court, would seriously undermine the importance of the case.

Significantly, Roberts began his argument with Madison's famous statement that "the accumulation of all powers, legislative, executive, and judiciary, in the same hands...may justly be pronounced the very definition of tyranny." Then he continued: "Although modern administrative agencies fit most comfortably within the Executive Branch, as a practical matter they exercise legislative power, by promulgating regulations with the force of law; executive power, by policing compliance with those regulations; and judicial power, by adjudicating enforcement and imposing sanctions on those found to have violated their rules."[16] Then: "It would be a bit much to describe the result as 'the very definition of tyranny,' but the danger posed by the growing power of the administrative state cannot be dismissed."[17] And, finally, quoting Marshall in *Marbury*, "It is emphatically the province and duty of the judicial department to say what the law is."[18]

Having laid this foundation, the Chief Justice then began to reinterpret and narrow *Chevron's* ostensible reach. First, he distinguished *Chevron* itself, saying that it involved only an issue about the "agency's policy," and since the courts stay out of policy issues "the agency...was the appropriate actor to resolve the competing interests at stake."[19] However, in general, before a court can give deference to an administrative agency's interpretation of its statutory authority, it must decide whether Congress "has in fact delegated to the agency lawmaking power over the ambiguity at issue."[20]

This appears to be a new and much narrower interpretation of *Chevron*, which had declared that where there was ambiguity in a statute the courts should *assume* that Congress had given the agency the authority to resolve it. If the courts were now required, in the Roberts analysis, to determine at the outset that Congress had given the agency the power it was attempting to invoke, this would put the courts back in the position of deciding whether Congress had granted the necessary power to the administrative agency. The courts—rather than the agency—would have the opportunity to decide "what the law is," perhaps precluding the agency from doing anything more than what the specific statutory language permitted. To remove all doubt, Roberts's dissent ended with this: "We do not leave it to the agency to decide when it is in charge."[21]

These very words were quoted by Justice Kennedy in concurring with an 8–1 decision by the Court in *Pereira v. Sessions*, decided on June 21, 2018. Kennedy (who was to announce his retirement only a week later) expressed concern that lower courts had too easily fallen back on *Chevron* deference when they should have made an effort to interpret the words of the statute—calling this "reflexive deference." Noting concerns about deference among other justices, including Roberts, Thomas, Alito, and Gorsuch, Kennedy then continued: "It seems necessary and appropriate to reconsider, in an appropriate case, the premises that underlie *Chevron*, and how courts have implemented that decision."[22]

City of Arlington and *Pereira*, then, suggest that there are at least four justices (Kennedy having retired), and possibly a fifth, if Judge Kavanaugh is confirmed, who may be willing to reconsider the Court's *Chevron* jurisprudence when an appropriate case arrives at the Court.

This conclusion is supported by the concurring opinions of Justices Scalia and Thomas in the 2015 case *Perez v. Mortgage Bankers Association*. The decision in the case was unanimous, with all justices agreeing that the Administrative Procedure Act did not require an administrative agency to use the notice-and-comment procedure when it issues a new interpretation of an existing regulation. Justices Alito, Scalia, and Thomas concurred in the result, but with different concurring opinions.

Scalia's opinion is the most interesting because it suggests that despite his long support for *Chevron* deference—and his fierce defense of the idea in *City of Arlington*—he was beginning to move closer to the Roberts view in *City of Arlington*. He signaled this by invoking the Administrative Procedure Act, which—although previously ignored by the Court in pressing forward with *Chevron*—seems to contradict the *Chevron* position that submerged judicial review in favor of deference:

> [T]he [APA] provides that "the *reviewing court* shall...interpret constitutional and statutory provisions, and determine the meaning or applicability of the terms of an agency action." [Emphasis added by Scalia.] The Act thus contemplates that courts, not agencies, will authoritatively resolve ambiguities in statutes and regulations.... An agency may use interpretive rules to *advise* the public by explaining its interpretation of the law. But an agency may not use interpretive rules to *bind* the public by making law, because it remains the responsibility of the court to decide whether the law means what the agency says it means.
>
> Heedless of the original design of the APA, we have developed an elaborate law of deference to agencies' interpretations of statutes and regulations. Never mentioning [the APA's] directive that the "reviewing court...interpret...statutory provisions," we have held that *agencies* may authoritatively resolve ambiguities in statutes [citing *Chevron*].[23]

Justice Thomas wrote a long concurrence to the same effect, but with more specific references to the separation of powers and the inconsistency of the Court's deference jurisprudence with the constitutional structure:

I write separately because these cases call into question the legitimacy of our precedents requiring deference to administrative interpretations of regulations. That line of precedents, beginning with *Bowles v. Seminole Rock*..., requires judges to defer to agency interpretations of regulations, thus, as happened in these cases, giving legal effect to the interpretations rather than the regulations themselves. Because this doctrine effects a transfer of the judicial power to an executive agency, it raises constitutional concerns. This line of precedents undermines our obligation to provide a *judicial check on the other branches*, and it subjects regulated parties to precisely the abuses that the Framers sought to prevent....

We have not always been vigilant about protecting the structure of our Constitution. Although this Court has repeatedly invoked the "separation of powers" and "the constitutional system of checks and balances" as core principles of our constitutional design, essential to the protection of individual liberty..., it has also endorsed a "more pragmatic, flexible approach" to that design when it has seemed more convenient to permit the powers to be mixed.... As the history shows, that approach runs the risk of compromising our constitutional structure.[24]

This language strongly suggests that Justice Thomas will be a fourth vote for a modification of *Chevron*, if the issue is properly presented to the Court. If he accepts the premise that the constitutional structure is "essential to the protection of liberty," it is difficult to imagine that he will later support a precedent that "effects a transfer of the judicial power to an executive agency."

In addition, Justice Gorsuch, as an appellate judge, recognized exactly the point made in this book: "What would happen," he mused in a 2016 decision, "in a world without *Chevron*?"

If this goliath of modern administrative law were to fall? Surely Congress could and would continue to pass statutes for administrative agencies to enforce. And just as surely agencies could and would continue to offer guidance on how they intend to enforce those statutes. The only difference would be that courts would then fulfill their duty to exercise their independent judgment about what the law *is*. Of course courts could and would consult agency views and apply the agency's interpretation when it accords with the best reading of a statute. But *de novo* judicial review of the law's meaning would limit the ability of an agency to alter and amend existing law.[25]

Assuming that this view is representative of the positions he will take as a member of the Supreme Court, Justice Gorsuch would have to be considered as a vote—and possibly a fifth vote—for a substantial modification of *Chevron* along the lines of the Roberts dissent in *City of Arlington*. If there were any doubt about Justice Gorsuch's view, it should be resolved by the opening paragraph of the separate concurring opinion he wrote in *Gutierrez-Brizuela v. Lynch*:

> There's an elephant in the room with us today. We have studiously attempted to work our way around it and even left it unremarked. But the fact is *Chevron* and *Brand X* permit executive bureaucracies to swallow huge amounts of core judicial and legislative power and concentrate federal power in a way that seems more than a little difficult to square with the Constitution of the framers' design. Maybe the time has come to face the behemoth.[26]

Finally, if Judge Kavanaugh is confirmed as a Supreme Court justice, he will almost certainly join the four justices who have already expressed concern about the effect of *Chevron*. His dissent in the net neutrality case discussed earlier was a strong endorsement of judicial review—the opposite of deference—although limited in that case to major decisions, a position arguably already articulated by the Supreme Court. If confirmed, he would have greater latitude to consider further limitations on *Chevron*. In the *Loan Syndication and Trading Association* case, discussed below, he joined two other appellate judges in a unanimous decision that denied deference to the SEC and Federal Reserve on the ground that the statutory language was clear. This was another endorsement of judicial review, and if adopted by the Supreme Court would significantly reduce the importance of *Chevron*.

Chief Justice Roberts's 2013 *City of Arlington* dissent may have created interest at the appellate-court level in finding ways to limit or avoid *Chevron*. That was the approach taken by the D.C. Circuit Court of Appeals in *The Loan Syndications and Trading Association v. Securities and Exchange Commission and Board of Governors of the Federal Reserve System*,[27] which could provide a template for how courts could reduce the application of *Chevron* without directly overturning it. The case arose under a provision of the 2010 Dodd-Frank Act, which, in the wake of the 2008 financial crisis, sought to impose caution and prudence on "securitizers" of financial assets by requiring them to retain some portion of the credit risk in any portfolio they securitized. The idea was to ensure that securitizers have "skin in the game" when they issue asset-backed securities.

Under this statutory provision the SEC and the Federal Reserve adopted regulations that covered firms engaged in loan syndication, and the association of such firms brought suit to prevent the application of these regulations to their members. This was a clear issue of statutory interpretation, in which the administrative agencies interpreted the statutory language to cover loan syndications in addition to asset securitizations. The agencies argued that they were entitled to deference: first, because Congress had left to them the task of interpreting the terms of the statute, and second—assuming the statutory language was ambiguous—because *Chevron* required that the courts defer to a "reasonable" interpretation by the agencies, which they of course had made.

Writing for a unanimous panel (Circuit Judge Brett Kavanaugh and Senior Circuit Judges Stephen Williams and Douglas Ginsburg), Judge Williams addressed *Chevron* at the outset—whether the agencies were entitled to deference in their interpretation of the statutory language. The court disposed of this argument quickly, noting that while a "reasonable agency interpretation prevails" under the *Chevron* precedent, "'if Congress has directly spoken to an issue then any agency interpretation contradicting what Congress has said would be unreasonable.'"[28] This was a restatement of the first step in analysis specified in the *Chevron* opinion: "If Congress has directly spoken on an issue, that is the end of the matter." The court then went on to a careful review of the statutory language and determined that Congress did not intend to cover the activities of loan syndicators. This made the administrative interpretation prima facie unreasonable—and thus outside the ambit of *Chevron*—because Congress had spoken on the issue.

This analysis, if eventually followed by the Supreme Court, would open up to traditional judicial review many cases that have previously been considered suitable for *Chevron* deference. The reviewing court can interpret the words of the statute, and if the court determines as an initial matter that Congress did not intend through that language to grant the authority the agency has claimed, then the agency's decision is by definition unreasonable and not entitled to *Chevron* deference. Once again, this puts the law as enacted by Congress above the rulings of administrative agencies, and returns the judicial process to the superior position that the Framers had in mind. If the case is followed by other courts, it promises to revive the importance of judicial review in administrative law. Even more important, if the case is appealed, it could be the vehicle for terminating or modifying *Chevron* and restoring the rule of law.

Another case, this time from the Fifth Circuit, seems to have taken a similar route. That decision involved the Department of Labor's so-called fiduciary rule, which labeled as fiduciaries those who advised pension fund investors about the specific investments that should be made in their accounts. The court did a thorough analysis of the department's interpretation of the applicable statute and, over a claim by the department that it was entitled to *Chevron* deference, concluded in a 2–1 decision that Congress had not authorized this interpretation. Therefore, having failed in *Chevron* step 1—what the *Chevron* Court said would be the "end of the matter"—the department was not entitled to deference on its determination.[29] This could be another case that, if appealed to the Supreme Court, could give the Court an opportunity to establish a new position on *Chevron*.

The *Chevron* Court's argument that administrative agencies have a closer relationship than the courts' to the electoral process—and hence by implication more legitimacy than the courts for interpreting laws—entirely misses the key point that under the Framers' design the courts were to determine whether the other branches stayed within their allotted channels. Similarly, the argument that administrative agencies are better interpreters of what Congress intended is also beside the point.

The judiciary's role in making sure that Congress and the executive branch stay within their allotted channels, as discussed in chapter 2, was part of a two-part process that the Framers set up to ensure that the constitutional structure was not changed over time. The other part—on the authoritative testimony of Madison in *Federalist* No. 51—comprised the checks and balances among the three branches, with the assumption by the Framers that each of the branches would selfishly guard its own prerogatives within the constitutional structure. In the *Chevron* matter, however, the Court has handed its birthright to the administrative state.

Today, the fail-safe devices in the APA and the Constitution seem in fact to have failed. Congress, as discussed in chapter 3, is no longer complaining when the executive assumes a number of the powers that Congress was intended to perform, and the judiciary seems intimidated by the fact that it does not have a mandate from the electorate. It was not supposed to. Cynthia Farina summarizes the issue well:

> If we remain committed to separation of powers as a central struc-
> tural credo, then choices such as the one made in *Chevron* are steps
> in the wrong direction. At stake in *Chevron* was the fate of one rel-
> atively small but not insignificant slice of the regulatory power pie:
> the authority to interpret the statutes that define the policy-mak-
> ing universe. The Court's resolution deliberately moves the power
> squarely into the President's domain. By relinquishing the authority
> to determine statutory "meaning" to agencies whenever Congress has
> failed to speak clearly and precisely, *Chevron* enlarges the quantum
> of administrative discretion potentially amenable to direction from
> the White House. It then goes even further and exhorts agencies to
> exercise this discretion, *not* by attempting to intuit and realize the
> objectives of the statute's enactors, but by pursuing the regulatory
> agenda of the current Chief Executive.[30]

What the *Chevron* Court Could Have Done

In the discussion above, I suggested that the Court in *Chevron* could have dealt with the case much more simply by saying that whether a "station-ary source" was a single building or a complex of buildings operated by the same company was a detail that was well within the authority of the

EPA to decide. This would not have been a very controversial decision, except with the NRDC, and would not have given a major boost to the agencies of the administrative state. After a decision like that, courts and counsel would have been sensitive to the issue of whether Congress had made the important decisions in any statute and left the details to the agency.

But what if the court in *Chevron* thought that the definition of stationary source *was* an important question—one that should be resolved by Congress? If—as seems likely—reinstating the nondelegation doctrine is a bridge too far for the Court at this point, an intermediate step, short of striking down a statute, might be useful to the courts as well as Congress. Some of these ideas are considered below.

First, if there is a lower court decision, the appellate court can remand the case for further determination of what Congress intended. In *Industrial Union Dept., AFL-CIO v. American Petroleum Institute* (1980), the Supreme Court could not agree on what authority had actually been delegated under the Occupational Safety and Health Act,[31] so the Court sent it back to the appellate court for remand to OSHA with instructions to start over while avoiding the use of "excessive discretion."

Second, confronted with an ambiguous statute and an agency's effort—as in *Chevron*—to reconcile conflicting interests, the court could say that it wants a clearer statement from Congress before enforcing the regulation.[32] Another possibility is that the court might remand the regulation to the administrative agency, requiring it to put the unresolved question before Congress for a vote.

Congress might even enact a procedure for an expedited treatment of such a request. This would be most appropriate, for example, under the facts of *Chevron*, in that the EPA could simply have asked Congress what it had in mind when it used the term "stationary source," a bubble concept or a single plant—or whether it would object if the agency adopted the bubble concept.

Another way to do this would be for the agency to put before Congress—*sua sponte* or at the instance of a court—its intention to adopt a particular interpretation of an ambiguity in a statute. If Congress does not act within a certain period, the agency's interpretation would be deemed correct by the courts.

The true value of any of these ideas would be as a disciplinary system for Congress, short of a finding that Congress had unlawfully delegated some of its legislative power or deliberately adopted ambiguous statutory language because it couldn't agree or—as the *Chevron* Court posited—it wanted an administrative agency to resolve a problem that was too difficult for Congress. If the courts were to send a sufficient number of disputed questions back to Congress for resolution, Congress might find that it is more expeditious to resolve some of these ambiguities when they first deal with the issue. For reasons outlined earlier, this would prevent later litigation challenging the agency's decision.

In any event, if we respect the Constitution's separation of powers, and the reason it was adopted by the Framers, some way must be found to restore a system in which Congress makes the laws and the executive branch carries them out. If the nondelegation doctrine is not to be revived, and *Chevron* is not modified, then something else has to be done to curb the growth of the administrative state. It is hard to say that we live in the democratic republic the Framers established when we have no effective control over how the laws we live under are made by people we did not elect.

CONCLUSION

The uncontrolled administrative state in place today is largely the result of the judiciary's failure to discharge its responsibilities under the checks and balances structure that the Framers designed. As outlined in this book, the judiciary's vital role began with ratification of the Constitution, was challenged during the Progressive Era, briefly asserted itself during the New Deal, and was finally submerged with the 1984 *Chevron* decision. There are indications today that a majority of the Court may be willing to reclaim some of these constitutional duties.

In his famous 1803 decision in *Marbury v. Madison,* Chief Justice Marshall further elucidated the judiciary's role by declaring not only that the courts could rule on whether a law was constitutional but also that "[i]t is emphatically the province and duty of the judicial department to say what the law is"—an idea bolstered 143 years later by the language of the Administrative Procedure Act. This means that the judiciary—and not the agencies themselves—should decide what Congress intended in the laws it enacts, and thus specifically what powers Congress conferred on administrative agencies. The fact that the judiciary has failed to do this routinely since 1935—indeed, going the other way with *Chevron* deference in 1984—accounts for the growth of the administrative state. A decision by the Supreme Court that simply endorses the idea that the courts "say what the law is" will restore the rule of law, reduce regulation that Congress has not specifically authorized, and put Congress back in charge of establishing the nation's most important policies.

The Framers saw clearly that the judiciary was a necessary element in the checks and balances system they had devised, principally to keep the other two branches—the legislature and the executive—in their assigned roles. It was the Framers' well-founded belief that, if both legislative and executive powers were ever united in a single person or group, the people's liberty would be in jeopardy. Indeed, that is one of the principal concerns shared by many conservatives and others about the administrative state—that these agencies have both the power to make laws and the power to enforce them. A scenario in which they also have the power to interpret the laws, as the *Chevron* case suggests, would be the Framers' nightmare.

Although some may believe that the Framers' constitutional structure is inadequate for the complexities of the modern world, there is little evidence for this. Woodrow Wilson thought the Constitution was too rigid to accommodate change, but that assessment turned out to be wrong. Here we are in the complex modern world, the U.S. constitutional system is still in place, and the United States has become the world's only superpower. If there is a problem with the government of the United States it is the ultrapartisanship of this era—the factional squabbling and inability to compromise that hampers the functioning of government—but that is not the fault of the constitutional structure. Indeed, it is a signature of a vigorous democracy and was also present even in the simpler world of the early nineteenth century. The government forms that have served the country well for more than two centuries are still in place, awaiting the political leaders or an event that can bring the warring parties together.

The better question is whether coping with the complexities of the modern world requires that key policy decisions for society must be left to the agencies of the administrative state. This idea is recited—often without challenge or logical support—by many academics and students of administrative law. The first response is to wonder whether administrators, in which the Progressives placed such confidence, have actually exhibited the skills their supporters assume. In chapter 4 I described the disappointment of the Progressives as they saw the agencies they had created in action. And in chapter 5 I described the many cases in which the regulations adopted by these supposedly skilled administrators made a mess of the industries—railroad, trucking, air travel, and securities—that they were regulating. It was only after repeal of those regulations and (in some cases) the closing down of the agencies themselves that competition was allowed to return to these industries, and consumers began to receive better services at lower prices. Competition, it seems, was a better regulator than a government agency.

Because these agencies were charged with regulating many different industries, they would clearly be required to deal with the complexities of the modern world as reflected in these industries. Yet, by any standard, they failed. In each case, Congress had handed them broad mandates, which they were unable to pursue successfully. These facts cast serious doubt on the claim that agencies of the administrative state are necessary to deal with the complexities of the modern world, and the proponents of administrative power should be required to demonstrate—with facts, not assertions[1]—exactly where complexity has made administrative agencies necessary.

Obviously, administrative agencies, including the major cabinet departments, are necessary to carry out the laws, and have been from the very outset of the government in the eighteenth century; the question addressed in this book is whether these agencies should have—as they do under *Chevron*—the power to make the major decisions for society, or whether they should simply carry out the specific authority that Congress gives them, as determined by the courts.

Perhaps the argument is not that administrative agencies are necessary to cope with modern complexity but that Congress cannot cope with complexity; therefore, the argument might run, the only viable governmental system is what we have today, with Congress providing broad authority to administrative agencies to "fix things" and the agencies taking it from there. In that case, despite the failure of these agencies, they are the only solution to a Congress boggled by the complexity of modern problems.

However, there is little evidence that Congress is unable to deal with this complexity. Congress can and does delegate technical matters for investigation and rulemaking by administrative agencies. In doing so, it ordinarily sets the parameters within which the agencies must work. A case in point is the highly complex tax legislation that passed both the House and Senate at the end of 2017. The fact that it was enacted with the support of only one party is irrelevant, just as it was irrelevant that the Affordable Care Act and the Dodd-Frank Act were both enacted by the House and Senate with the support of only one party. It would be better, of course, for major legislation to be passed on a bipartisan basis, but the fact that these laws were not is not a result of their complexity.

In other words, Congress can get complex things done when it wants to and does not need the administrative state to handle difficult problems.

The challenge for Congress today is not complexity but the difficulty of finding agreement on controversial questions. Here we come to the nub of the issue. If Congress cannot agree on a solution to a highly controversial issue, the proper course is not to turn the problem over to an administrative agency. An unelected bureaucracy has no legitimacy for making decisions of that kind, and if Congress adopts this course, the courts should declare it an unconstitutional delegation of legislative authority. Administrative agencies must be given standards on which to base decisions, not merely goals. It is far better to leave issues unresolved than to resolve them in a way that deprives the American people of a voice in the resolution. This does not mean giving the voters what they want but ensuring that a legitimate political process considers and weighs their views. Waiting for Congress to find the right answer may mean that many issues will go unresolved for a time, but that is the price of democracy. Conversely, allowing an administrative agency to make a major decision that is the province of Congress will certainly destroy the decision's legitimacy.

In a somewhat startling Monmouth University poll published in January 2018, almost 80 percent of respondents said "it is more important for Congress to make sure it has open hearings and gets input from a wide variety of interests *even if that means some of the policies the survey participants personally support may not get passed....*" Moreover, when asked about specific issues, "the vast majority of the public still says it would prefer to see Congress use 'regular order' to consider bills even if it means that they might not individually agree with the outcome. This includes tax policies (78%), health care policies (75%), gun policies (72%), and abortion policies (71%)."[2]

This is a remarkable vote in favor of U.S. democracy as it is conceived, although not necessarily how it actually functions today; for years, by wide margins, polls have shown that the American people believe the country is headed in the wrong direction. Nevertheless, the public still shows strong support for the *process* by which the laws are made. In fact, the political process seems to be more important to them than the laws themselves.

Chief Justice William Rehnquist grasped very early in his career on the Court that the laws confer moral authority because they are made through a political process: "It is the fact of their enactment that gives them whatever moral claim they have upon us as a society...and not any independent virtue they may have in any particular citizen's own scale of values."[3] This statement is virtually a summary of the Monmouth poll, over forty years in advance. It is also a powerful reason why the laws should be read and enforced as they were written; an administrative reinterpretation of the laws at a later time reduces their moral authority and thus their legitimacy.

The sense that unelected officials, and not an elected Congress, are making the crucial decisions for society has produced a growing sense of illegitimacy surrounding the administrative state. The fear expressed by some scholars and other observers that the courts might act in a countermajoritarian way has turned out to be aimed at the wrong target. It is the administrative state that is failing to persuade large numbers of Americans that it has the right to set the rules they have to live under. This is understandable, because most Americans want less regulation and more freedom—an aspiration that is wholly inconsistent with the normal aspirations of administrators. If freedom is being restricted, the American people want to know that it is being done in a legitimate way.

What all this suggests is that the American people, if anything, want more democracy, more input into the political process, and a more engaged Congress. Necessarily, then, what they do not want are decisions made for them by an unelected and opaque bureaucracy: the very definition of the administrative state. If the country continues along the path on which it is currently embarked, a Brexit-like crisis of legitimacy is certainly in our future.

As noted in the introduction to this book, Brexit was the result of the European Union's failure to retain the confidence of the British people. There were many issues swirling in the Brexit debate, including the sensitive issue of immigration, but that is exactly the point. Just as Americans find moral authority in laws that are made in a democratic political process, it can be assumed that our British cousins felt the same way. They voted to leave the EU because they did not like the process by which the policies of the EU on immigration and other matters were made, just as an overwhelming majority of Americans in the Monmouth poll want the nation's fundamental policies to be made by Congress in an open political process, even if the outcome is not to their liking. To the British voters, the EU's rules did not have moral authority because they were not made in a democratic way. Regulations emanating from Brussels, unreflective of the British people's will, turned the British people against the EU.

Two points about the U.S. Constitution are important here: it does not lack legitimacy—that is, massive majorities of the American people believe it is just—and it has a mechanism for change built into it. If it ever happens that the American people want a different system, they have the unquestioned power to revise it. Until that time, however, those who doubt its value should concentrate on changing it in the ways the Constitution provides, not by handing power to an unelected bureaucracy because they believe its decisions will be better than those of the Congress or the courts.

There are really only two choices. Allow things to go on as they have been, with more and more power concentrated in a faceless bureaucracy in Washington, or revive the system the Framers created to protect our freedoms. For the first, we have only to sit back and watch it happen. For the second, we must imbue the judiciary with the fortitude the Framers expected from independent judges.

Acknowledgments

The idea for this book has been germinating for quite a while, and I have been discussing it with many friends and colleagues. All of these discussions have been helpful, but in particular I want to thank three friends who took the time to write to me about the broad themes I was considering: Ken Manaster, a college and law school classmate, now an emeritus professor at Santa Clara University; Si Lazarus, a college classmate and a constitutional law specialist in Washington, D.C.; and Joel Gora, a professor at Brooklyn Law School and coauthor of our book on campaign finance reform. I don't want to suggest that any of them necessarily agree with what I've chosen to write, but their candid thoughts were a great help to me in framing the arguments.

I also want to thank my former assistant at AEI, Ryan Nabil, for his research assistance on many issues and the development of some of the numerical data about the growth of government that are used in the book. Many other members of the AEI staff have been helpful, and the support of AEI itself—a remarkable institution with which I've been fortunate to be associated for almost twenty years—has been invaluable. Jessica Hornik Evans, the book's copyeditor, took a rather randomly cited and quoted text and turned it into a consistent piece of scholarship.

Finally, I want to thank my wife, Frieda, a superb lawyer, for reading through and editing the manuscript—and pointing out, gently, the many places where I had missed the mark. My love goes with my thanks.

Notes

INTRODUCTION

1 For this and all other quotations from the *Federalist Papers*, see the Avalon Project: Documents in Law, History and Diplomacy, http://avalon.law.yale.edu/subject_menus/fed.asp.

2 Marbury v. Madison, 5 U.S. 137, 177 (1803).

3 John Locke, *Second Treatise of Government* (1689), http://www.earlymoderntexts.com/assets/pdfs/locke1689a.pdf.

4 Panama Refining Co. v. Ryan, 293 U.S. 388 (1935), and A.L.A. Schechter Poultry Corp. v. United States, 295 U.S. 495 (1935).

5 Whether the "switch in time" was actually induced by the court-packing plan is hotly debated among legal scholars. An interesting and thorough review of the issue—concluding that a change in Justice Roberts's position was not induced by the court-packing plan—is found in Daniel E. Ho and Kevin M. Quinn, "Did the Switch in Time Save Nine?" *Journal of Legal Analysis* 2, no. 1 (2010): 69–113.

6 Mark Tushnet, "Administrative Law in the 1930s: The Supreme Court's Accommodation of Progressive Legal Theory," *Duke Law Journal* 60 (2011): 1624. Tushnet quotes FCC v. Pottsville Broadcasting Co., 309 U.S. 134, 142 (1940).

7 Chevron U.S.A. Inc. v. Natural Resources Defense Council, Inc., 467 U.S. 837, 866 (1984) (quoting TVA v. Hill, 437 U.S. 153, 195 [1978].)

8 United States v. Nichols, 784 F. 3d 666, 671 (10th Cir. 2015).

9 Gutierrez-Brizuela v. Lynch, 834 F. 3d 1142 (10 Cir. 2016).

10 Clyde Wayne Crews Jr., *Ten Thousand Commandments: An Annual Snapshot of the Federal Regulatory State—2018 Edition*, Competitive Enterprise Institute (April 19, 2018), 5, https://cei.org/10kc2018.

11 Boris Johnson, "The Risks of Remain: Democracy," June 6, 2016, http://www.voteleavetakecontrol.org/voting_to_stay_in_the_eu_is_the_risky_option.html.

12 Crews, *Ten Thousand Commandments*, 4. https://cei.org/10kc2018.

13 See, e.g., United States v. Carolene Products, 304 U.S. 144 (1938).

14 Charles Murray, *By the People: Rebuilding Liberty Without Permission* (New York: Crown Forum, 2015).

15 City of Arlington, TX v. FCC, 569 U.S. 290, 327 (2013) (emphasis added).

CHAPTER 1: THE ADMINISTRATIVE STATE AND THE RULE OF LAW

1 F. A. Hayek, *The Road to Serfdom: Text and Documents, the Definitive Edition*, ed. Bruce Caldwell (Chicago: University of Chicago Press, 2007), 119.

2 Hayek, *The Road to Serfdom*, 118.

3 Perez v. Mortgage Bankers Association, 135 S. Ct 1199, 1223 (2015).

4 The relevant section of the act provides: (d) ABUSIVE.—The Bureau shall have no authority under this section to declare an act or practice abusive in connection with the provision of a consumer financial product or service, unless the act or practice—(1) materially interferes with the ability of a consumer to understand a term or condition of a consumer financial product or service; or (2) takes unreasonable advantage of—(A) a lack of understanding on the part of the consumer of the material risks, costs, or conditions of the product or service; (B) the inability of the consumer to protect the interests of the consumer in selecting or using a consumer financial product or service; or (C) the reasonable reliance by the consumer on a covered person to act in the interests of the consumer.

5 Dave Clarke, "US Abusive Lending Bar Likely Set High: Cordray," Reuters (January 24, 2012), https://www.reuters.com/article/idINL2E8COFA620120124.

6 Mick Mulvaney, Memorandum to the staff of the CFPB (January 23, 2018), https://www.documentcloud.org/documents/4357880-Mulvaney-Memo.html.

7 Todd J. Zywicki, "The Consumer Financial Protection Bureau: Savior or Menace?" George Washington Law Review 81, no. 3 (2013): 922.

8 Neomi Rao, "Administrative Collusion: How Delegation Diminishes the Collective Congress," New York University Law Review 90, no. 5 (2015): 1490.

9 Mulvaney memorandum, 2018.

10 Alexander v. Yale University, 459 F. Supp. 1 (D. Conn. 1977).

11 R. Shep Melnick, The Transformation of Title IX: Regulating Gender Equality in Education (Washington, DC: Brookings Institution Press), 2018, 43.

12 Melnick, The Transformation of Title IX, 44.

13 Melnick, The Transformation of Title IX, 186.

14 Davis v. Monroe County Board of Education, 526 U.S. 629 (1999).

15 U.S. Department of Education, Office of Civil Rights, "Sexual Harassment: It's Not Academic," September 2008, https://www2.ed.gov/about/offices/list/ocr/docs/ocrshpam.html.

16 Resolution Agreement Among the University of Montana-Missoula, the U.S. Department of Justice, Civil Rights Division, Educational Opportunities Section and the U.S. Department of Education, Office of Civil Rights, May 2013, 2, https://www.justice.gov/sites/default/files/crt/legacy/2013/05/09/montanaagree.pdf.

17 U.S. Department of Justice, Civil Rights Division, and U.S. Department of Education, Office for Civil Rights, letter to President Royce Engstrom of the University of Montana, May 9, 2013, 9, https://www.justice.gov/sites/default/files/opa/legacy/2013/05/09/um-ltr-findings.pdf.

18 For a good summary, see David B. Rivkin Jr. and Elizabeth Price Foley, "Five Ways to Restore the Separation of Powers," Wall Street Journal (December 19, 2016). In By the People, Murray lists many instances in which the Obama administration acted unilaterally without congressional authorization, and twenty times when its actions were rejected 9-0 by the Supreme Court. Many of these Obama defeats were listed in memoranda by Senator Ted Cruz, a former Supreme Court clerk. Some of the Cruz claims have been disputed, and I will not try to litigate the issue here. One of the boldest actions taken by the Obama White House was to use funds for the

2010 Affordable Care Act that had not been specifically appropriated for that purpose by Congress, thus skirting one of the fundamental powers of Congress under the Constitution. The House of Representatives challenged this in *U.S. House of Representatives v. Burwell*, and its right to challenge the administration's action was upheld by the D.C. Federal District Court. The decision was not appealed before the end of the Obama administration.

19 Sec 1831p-1 of the U.S. Code.

20 U.S. House of Representatives, Committee of Oversight and Government Reform, "Federal Deposit Insurance Corporation's Involvement in 'Operation Choke Point,'" Staff Report, 113th Congress (December 8, 2014), 3.

21 Advance America, Cash Advance Centers, Inc. v. FDIC, 251 F.Supp.3d 78 (2017).

22 Massachusetts v. Environmental Protection Agency, 549 U.S. 497 (2007).

23 Utility Air Regulatory Group v. Environmental Protection Agency et al., 134 S. Ct. 2427, 2445 (2014).

24 *Utility Air*, 134 S. Ct. at 2446.

25 *Utility Air*, 134 S. Ct. at 2451.

26 The key provision of the act reads as follows: "(a) Employer practices. It shall be an unlawful employment practice for an employer— (1) to fail or refuse to hire or to discharge any individual, or otherwise to discriminate against any individual with respect to his compensation, terms, conditions, or privileges of employment, because of such individual's race, color, religion, sex, or national origin; or (2) to limit, segregate, or classify his employees or applicants for employment in any way which would deprive or tend to deprive any individual of employment opportunities or otherwise adversely affect his status as an employee, because of such individual's race."

27 Griggs v. Duke Power Company, 401 U.S. 424 (1971).

28 *Griggs*, 401 U.S. at 433.

29 Texas Dept. of Housing and Community Affairs v. Inclusive Communities Project, Inc., 135 S. Ct. 2507 (2015).

30 *Texas Dept. of Housing and Community Affairs*, 135 S. Ct. at 2526.

31 *Texas Dept. of Housing and Community Affairs*, 135 S. Ct. at 2526, citing Ricci v. DeStefano, 557 U.S. 557, 577 (2009).

32 "Clean Water Rule: Definition of 'Waters of the United States,'" *Federal Register* (June 29, 2015), https://www.federalregister.gov/documents/2015/06/29/2015-13435/clean-water-rule-definition-of-waters-of-the-united-states.

33 Food and Drug Administration v. Brown & Williamson Tobacco Corp., 529 U.S. 120, 155–159 (2000).

34 F. A. Hayek, *The Constitution of Liberty: The Definitive Edition*, ed. Ronald Hamowy (Chicago: University of Chicago Press, 2011), 214.

CHAPTER 2: THE SEPARATION OF POWERS AND CHECKS AND BALANCES

1 Concurring in Perez v. Mortgage Bankers Association, 135 S. Ct. 1199, 2021 (2015).

2 Sessions v. Dimaya, 584 U.S. _____ (2018).

3 Richard A. Epstein, *The Classical Liberal Constitution: The Uncertain Quest for Limited Government* (Cambridge, MA: Harvard University Press, 2014), 570.

4 Walter Berns, "Ancients and Moderns: The Emergence of Modern Constitutionalism," in *Democracy and the Constitution: Essays* (Washington, DC: AEI Press, 2006), 14.

5 Berns, "Ancients and Moderns," 114–115.

6 *Marbury*, 5 U.S. at 177.

7 *Sessions v. Dimaya*, quoting Justice Robert Jackson's dissent in Jordan v. De George, 341 U.S. 223 (1951).

8 The logic of this is obviously faulty, since it is highly likely that Congress— if presented with the idea that CO_2 is an air pollutant—would have rejected it. CO_2 is a naturally occurring gas, produced by animals and volcanoes, and essential to plant life. It thus defies classification as a pollutant.

9 Frank H. Easterbrook, "Statutes' Domains," *University of Chicago Law Review* 50 (1983): 551.

10 *Utility Air*, 134 S. Ct. at 2453.

11 Felix Frankfurter, "The Task of Administrative Law," *University of Pennsylvania Law Review* 75, no. 7 (1927): 614.

12 Walter Gellhorn, "The Administrative Agency—A Threat to Democracy?" in *Federal Administrative Proceedings* (Baltimore: The Johns Hopkins Press, 1941), 15 (emphasis added).

CHAPTER 3: CONGRESS AND THE ADMINISTRATIVE STATE

1 James Burnham, *Congress and the American Tradition* (Chicago: Regnery, 1965), 100.

2 Woodrow Wilson, *Congressional Government: A Study in American Politics* (Boston: Houghton Mifflin, 1885), 6.

3 Wilson, *Congressional Government*, 36.

4 Burnham, *Congress and the American Tradition*, 259.

5 Gerald Leonard, "Party as a 'Political Safeguard of Federalism': Martin Van Buren and the Constitutional Theory of Party Politics," *Rutgers Law Review* 54 (2001): 222.

6 Daryl J. Levinson and Richard H. Pildes, "Separation of Parties, Not Powers," *Harvard Law Review* 119, no. 8 (2006): 2333.

7 Levinson and Pildes, "Separation of Parties, Not Powers," 2341.

8 Congressional Research Service, "Memorandum: 'Major' Obama Administration Rules Potentially Eligible to Be Overturned under the Congressional Review Act in the 115th Congress" (November 17, 2016), https://fas.org/sgp/crs/misc/major-rules-cra.pdf.

9 Christopher DeMuth, "Can the Administrative State Be Tamed?" *Journal of Legal Analysis* 8, no. 1 (2016): 179.

10 See, e.g., Eric A. Posner and Adrian Vermeule, "Interring the Nondelegation Doctrine," *University of Chicago Law Review* 69 (2002): 1721–1762 ("A statutory grant of authority to the executive isn't a *transfer* of legislative power, but an *exercise* of legislative power"); Daryl J. Levinson, "Empire-Building Government in Constitutional Law," *Harvard Law Review* 118, no. 3 (2005): 915–972 ("Congressional control over agency structure, authority, and procedures, combined with the formidable investigatory resources of oversight and appropriations committees, should keep agencies much more in line with congressional preferences"); and Thomas

W. Merrill, "Rethinking Article I, Section I: From Nondelegation to
Exclusive Delegation," *Columbia Law Review* 104, no. 8 (2004): 2097–2181
("Congress has created the administrative state and has given its far-flung
agencies extensive powers to adopt legislative rules. But there is nothing
constitutionally problematic about this if Article I, Section I tells us not that
only Congress can legislate, but only Congress can delegate").

11 DeMuth, "Can the Administrative State Be Tamed?," 132.

12 Industrial Union Department, AFL-CIO v. American Petroleum Institute,
448 U.S. 607 (1980).

13 Telecommunications Act of 1996, Sec 254(h)(2)(A).

14 Texas Office of Public Utility Counsel v. Federal Communications
Commission, 183 F.3d 393 (5th Cir. 1999): "Under *Chevron* step-two, the
FCC has reasonably concluded that it can fulfill its statutory duty to
'designate' while giving schools and libraries the maximum flexibility to
choose which services they need. It is not unreasonable for the FCC to
conclude that it could best 'take into account...the particular needs' of
schools and libraries by allowing support for all commercially available
telecommunications services."

15 Author's files.

16 Rao, "Administrative Collusion," 1510.

17 PHH Corporation, et al. v. Consumer Financial Protection Bureau, 839 F.3d
1 (D.C. Cir. 2016). In January 2018 an *en banc* decision of the D.C. Circuit
determined that the appointment of the director of the CFPB for a five-year
term of office, with removal by the president only for malfeasance, was not
unconstitutional, overruling an earlier decision by a panel of the court. At
this writing, there has been no announcement whether this decision will be
appealed to the Supreme Court.

18 *Industrial Union*, 448 U.S. at 687.

CHAPTER 4: PROGRESSIVISM AND
THE RISE OF THE ADMINISTRATIVE STATE

1 Olmstead v. United States, 277 U.S. 438, 479 (1928).

2 Woodrow Wilson, *The New Freedom: A Call for the Emancipation of the
Generous Energies of a People* (Garden City, NY: Doubleday Page, 1913), 47.

3 Woodrow Wilson, *Constitutional Government in the United States* (New York:
Columbia University Press, 1911), 54.

4 Wilson, *Congressional Government*, 284.

5 Woodrow Wilson, "The Study of Administration," *Political Science Quarterly*
2, no. 2 (1887): 200–201.

6 Wilson, "The Study of Administration," 213–214.

7 In many ways, Theodore Roosevelt was more radical than Wilson,
advocating specific changes in the Constitution to make it more
majoritarian and responsive to public demands. See, e.g., Sidney M. Milkis,
*Theodore Roosevelt, the Progressive Party, and the Transformation of American
Democracy* (Lawrence: University Press of Kansas, 2009).

8 Herbert Hovenkamp, "The Mind and Heart of Progressive Legal Thought,"
Twelfth Annual Presidential Lecture, University of Iowa, (February 5, 1995),
9, http://ir.uiowa.edu/cgi/viewcontent.cgi?article=1020&context=
presidential-lecture-series.

9 Tushnet, "Administrative Law in the 1930s," 1568.

10 A good general discussion of Progressivism appears in Thomas C. Leonard, *Illiberal Reformers: Race, Eugenics, and American Economics in the Progressive Era* (Princeton, NJ: Princeton University Press, 2016).

11 Buck v. Bell, 274 U.S. 200, 207 (1927).

12 Leonard, *Illiberal Reformers*, 110.

13 In "The Reconstruction of the Southern States," printed in the *Atlantic Monthly* in January 1901, Wilson wrote that Jim Crow was necessary in the South because without it black Americans "were a danger to themselves as well as to those whom they had once served."

14 Michael McGerr, *A Fierce Discontent: The Rise and Fall of the Progressive Movement in America, 1870–1920* (New York: Free Press, 2003), 191–192.

15 An excellent and meticulously researched book that covers the Progressive Era is by my AEI colleague Jonah Goldberg, *Liberal Fascism: The Secret History of the American Left from Mussolini to the Politics of Meaning* (New York: Doubleday, 2007).

16 Leonard, *Illiberal Reformers*, 10.

17 Wilson, *Congressional Government*, 13.

18 Wilson, "The Study of Administration," 216.

19 Ronald J. Pestritto, *Woodrow Wilson and the Roots of Modern Liberalism* (Lanham, MD: Rowman and Littlefield, 2005), 72.

20 Woodrow Wilson, *The State: Elements of Historical and Practical Politics*, rev. ed. (Boston: Heath, 1898), 631.

21 Ken I. Kersch, "Constitutional Conservatives Remember the Progressive Era," in *The Progressives' Century: Political Reform, Constitutional Government, and the Modern American State*, ed. Stephen Skowronek, Stephen M. Engel, and Bruce Ackerman (New Haven, CT: Yale University Press, 2016), 140.

22 Philip Hamburger, *Is Administrative Law Unlawful?* (Chicago: University of Chicago Press, 2014), 9 (emphasis added).

23 Leonard, *Illiberal Reformers*, x.

24 Herbert Hovenkamp, "Progressive Legal Thought," *Washington and Lee Law Review* 72, no. 2 (2015): 656–657.

25 Richard Hofstadter, *The Age of Reform: From Bryan to F.D.R.* (New York: Vintage, 1955), 283.

26 Felix Frankfurter, *The Public and Its Government* (New Haven, CT: Yale University Press, 1930). Also at https://archive.org/stream/in.ernet. dli.2015.264284/2015.264284.The-Public_djvu.txt.

27 Ironically, according to Milton Friedman and Anna Schwartz, in an analysis now widely accepted by economists, it was the misplaced policies of the Federal Reserve, a Progressive innovation, that caused and sustained the downturn in the economy that extended through the 1930s and powered the New Deal. See Milton Friedman and Anna Jacobson Schwartz, *A Monetary History of the United States, 1867–1960* (Princeton, NJ: Princeton University Press, 1971).

28 Oddly, Frankfurter, one of FDR's Progressive appointees to the Supreme Court, complained in *The Public and Its Government*, in 1930, that before that year "members of the Supreme Court continued to reflect the social and economic order in which they grew up."

29　Hovenkamp, "The Mind and Heart of Progressive Legal Thought," 9.

30　Hofstadter, *The Age of Reform*, 283.

31　Hofstadter, *The Age of Reform*, 284.

32　John Maynard Keynes, *The General Theory of Employment, Interest, and Money* (San Diego and New York: Harcourt, 1964), 383.

33　Kersch, "Constitutional Conservatives," 130.

34　Rexford Guy Tugwell, "America's Wartime Socialism," *The Nation* (April 6, 1927): 364–365.

35　James M. Landis, *The Administrative Process* (New Haven, CT: Yale University Press, 1938), 23–24.

36　Gerard C. Henderson, *The Federal Trade Commission: A Study in Administrative Law and Procedure* (New Haven, CT: Yale University Press, 1924), 328.

37　Frankfurter, *The Public and Its Government*, 119–120.

38　Tushnet, "Administrative Law in the 1930s," 1578.

39　Tushnet, "Administrative Law in the 1930s," 1583.

40　Tushnet, "Administrative Law in the 1930s," 1588–1589.

41　See, e.g., Daniel R. Ernst, *Tocqueville's Nightmare: The Administrative State Emerges in America, 1900–1940* (Oxford and New York: Oxford University Press, 2014).

42　Tushnet, "Administrative Law in the 1930s," 1590.

43　St. Joseph Stock Yards Co. v. United States 298 U.S. 38, 51–52. (1936).

44　Tushnet, "Administrative Law in the 1930s," 1591.

45　Gray v. Powell, 314 U.S. 402, 411–412 (1941)

46　*Gray v. Powell*, 314 U.S. at 417–418.

47　Epstein, *The Classical Liberal Constitution*, 34.

48　Emily Bazelon and Eric Posner, "The Government Gorsuch Wants to Undo," *New York Times* (April 1, 2017).

CHAPTER 5: WAS THE PROGRESSIVE FAITH
IN ECONOMIC REGULATION JUSTIFIED?

1　Ludwig von Mises, *The Anti-Capitalistic Mentality* (Auburn, AL: Mises Institute, 2008 [1956]), 99–100.

2　Adam Smith, *An Inquiry into the Nature and Causes of the Wealth of Nations*, ed. Edwin Cannon (London: Methuen, 1904 [1776]), bk. 1, chap 2., http://oll.libertyfund.org/titles/smith-an-inquiry-into-the-nature-and-causes-of-the-wealth-of-nations-cannan-ed-vol-1.

3　Steve Eder, "When Picking Apples on a Farm with 5,000 Rules, Watch Out for the Ladders," *New York Times* (December 27, 2017), https://www.nytimes.com/2017/12/27/business/picking-apples-on-a-farm-with-5000-rules-watch-out-for-the-ladders.html.

4　Mark J. Perry, "Fortune 500 Firms 1955 v. 2017: Only 60 Remain, Thanks to the Creative Destruction That Fuels Economic Prosperity," AEIdeas (October 20, 2017), http://www.aei.org/publication/fortune-500-firms-1955-v-2017-only-12-remain-thanks-to-the-creative-destruction-that-fuels-economic-prosperity/.

5　F. A. Hayek, "Competition as a Discovery Procedure," in *New Studies in Philosophy, Politics, Economics, and the History of Ideas* (London: Routledge and Kegan Paul, 1978).

6 Israel M. Kirzner, *Discovery and the Capitalist Process* (Chicago: University of Chicago Press, 1985), 141.

7 Gordon Tullock, Arthur Seldon, and Gordon L. Brady, *Government Failure: A Primer in Public Choice* (Washington, DC: Cato Institute, 2002), 11–12.

8 Kirzner, *Discovery and the Capitalist Process*, 142.

9 An excellent book on the history of bank regulation in the U.S. is Charles W. Calomiris, *U.S. Bank Deregulation in Historical Perspective* (New York: Cambridge University Press, 2000).

10 For general information, see Congressional Research Service, "Cost-Benefit and Other Analysis Requirements in the Rulemaking Process" (December 2014), https://fas.org/sgp/crs/misc/R41974.pdf.

11 Crews reports as follows on the only government report on regulatory costs, which he describes as deficient in several respects: "The vastness of the regulatory enterprise remains unknown, as there are numerous categories of untabulated costs. The only official reckoning citizens get today is an OMB annual survey of a subset of regulatory costs and benefits. The OMB's 2017 *Draft Report to Congress on the Benefits and Costs of Federal Regulations and Agency Compliance with the Unfunded Mandates Reform Act*, the most recent edition, only covers through FY 2015, despite being required annually by law. The report includes only a 10-year aggregate cost tabulation, when an aggregate one is required" (*Ten Thousand Commandments 2018*, 15).

12 Paul Krugman, "The Economic Fallout," *New York Times* (November 9, 2016).

13 David Shepardson and Valerie Volcovici, "White House Deregulation Push Clears Out Hundreds of Proposed Rules," Reuters (July 20, 2017), https://www.reuters.com/article/us-usa-trump-regulation/white-house-deregulation-push-clears-out-hundreds-of-proposed-rules-idUSKBN1A51O1.

14 Clyde Wayne Crews Jr., "The Tip of the Costberg" (October 2, 2014; rev. January 9, 2017), https://ssrn.com/abstract=2502883.

15 See Peter J. Wallison, *Hidden in Plain Sight: What Really Caused the World's Worst Financial Crisis and Why It Could Happen Again* (New York: Encounter Books, 2015).

16 Crews, "The Tip of the Costberg," and *Ten Thousand Commandments 2018*, 3. Crews's actual number is $1.9 trillion annually, but as he makes clear in the former work, this can only be a guess. The U.S. government, despite the fact that it imposes these costs, does virtually nothing to discover how much they are. Crews's number is almost certainly the best number anyone could come up with in an environment like this and, as he says, is likely to be low.

17 Mercatus Center, "The Impossibility of Comprehending, or Even Reading, All Federal Regulations" (October 23, 2017), https://www.mercatus.org/print/266634.

18 Bentley Coffey, Patrick A. McLaughlin, and Pietro Peretto, "The Cumulative Cost of Regulations," Mercatus Working Paper, April 2016, https://www.mercatus.org/system/files/Coffey-Cumulative-Cost-Regs-v3.pdf.

19 Coffey, McLaughlin, and Peretto, "The Cumulative Cost of Regulations," 7.

20 Terry Miller and Anthony B. Kim, *2017 Index of Economic Freedom*, Institute

for Economic Freedom, Heritage Foundation, 4, https://www.heritage.org/index/pdf/2017/book/index_2017.pdf.

21 Miller and Kim, *2017 Index of Economic Freedom*, 12.

22 Milton Friedman, *Capitalism and Freedom* (Chicago: University of Chicago Press, 2002 [1962]), 15.

23 R. H. Coase, "The Problem of Social Cost," *Journal of Law and Economics* 3 (October 1960): 34

24 Coase, "The Problem of Social Cost," 42 (emphasis added).

25 Geoffrey Brennan and James M. Buchanan, "Is Public Choice Immoral? The Case for the 'Nobel' Lie," in *The Collected Works of James M. Buchanan*, Vol. 13: *Politics as Public Choice* (Indianapolis, IN: Liberty Fund, 2000), 81.

26 James M. Buchanan, "The Achievement and the Limits of Public Choice in Diagnosing Government Failure and in Offering Bases for Constructive Reform," in *The Collected Works of James M. Buchanan*, Vol. 13: *Politics as Public Choice* (Indianapolis, IN: Liberty Fund, 2000), 113.

27 Buchanan, "The Achievement and the Limits of Public Choice," in *Collected Works*, Vol. 13, 118, 120.

28 Buchanan, "Politics and Meddlesome Preferences," in *Collected Works*, Vol. 13, 418.

29 Christopher DeMuth, "Can the Administrative State Be Tamed?" *Journal of Legal Analysis* 8, no. 1 (2016): 173.

30 Nancy L. Rose, "After Airline Deregulation and Alfred E. Kahn," *American Economic Review* 102, no. 3 (2012): 376.

31 Rose, "After Airline Deregulation and Alfred E. Kahn," 376, quoting Kahn.

32 Federal Railroad Administration, Office of Rail Policy and Development (March 2011), "Impact of the Staggers Rail Act of 1980," 1, https://www.fra.dot.gov/eLib/Details/L03012.

33 Thomas Gale Moore, "Trucking Deregulation," in *The Concise Encyclopedia of Economics* (1993), http://www.econlib.org/library/Enc1/TruckingDeregulation.html.

34 MIT, "Competition and Productivity in the US Trucking Industry Since Deregulation," US Transportation Productivity Study (2013), http://transportation.mit.edu/sites/default/files/documents/MIT_Trucking_Productivity_Report_2013.pdf.

35 Jason Zweig, "Lessons of May Day 1975 Ring True Today: The Intelligent Investor," *Wall Street Journal* (April 30, 2015), https://www.wsj.com/articles/lessons-of-may-day-1975-ring-true-today-the-intelligent-investor-1430450405.

36 Bruce M. Owen, "Net Neutrality and Title II of the Communications Act," SIEPR Policy Brief (January 2015), 1, https://siepr.stanford.edu/sites/default/files/publications/PolicyBrief-1-15-owen_0.pdf.

37 Federal Communications Commission, Fact Sheet: Restoring Internet Freedom (April 27, 2017), https://apps.fcc.gov/edocs_public/attachmatch/DOC-344614A1.pdf.

38 Epstein, *The Classical Liberal Constitution*, 40.

CHAPTER 6: THE NONDELEGATION DOCTRINE

1 In dissent, City of Arlington, TX v. FCC, 569 U.S. 290 (2013).

2 See, e.g., Gary Lawson, "Delegation and Original Meaning," *Virginia Law Review* 88, no. 2 (2002): 327–404.

3 See, e.g., Thomas W. Merrill, "Rethinking Article I, Section 1: From Nondelegation to Exclusive Delegation," *Columbia Law Review* 104, no. 8 (2004): 2097–2181.

4 Gillian E. Metzger, "The Supreme Court 2016 Term: 1930s Redux—The Administrative State Under Siege" (foreword), *Harvard Law Review* 131, no. 2 (2017): 2–95.

5 Crews, *Ten Thousand Commandments 2018*, 2.

6 *City of Arlington*, 569 U.S. at 313.

7 Wayman v. Southard, 23 U.S. 1, 42–45 (1825) (emphasis added).

8 Marshall Field & Co. v. Clark, 143 U.S. 649, 693 (1892) (emphasis added).

9 United States v. Grimaud, 220 U.S. 506, 516 (1911) (emphasis added).

10 J. W. Hampton, Jr., & Co. v. United States, 276 U.S. 394, 409 (1928) (emphasis added).

11 See, e.g., Touby v. United States, 500 U.S. 160 (1991), and Mistretta v. United States, 488 U.S. 361 (1989).

12 Concurring in Whitman v. American Trucking Assns, Inc., 531 U.S. 457 (2001).

13 Panama Refining Company v. Ryan, 293 U.S. 388, 415 (1935) (emphasis added).

14 *Panama Refining*, 293 U.S. at 428–429 (emphasis added).

15 A.L.A. Schechter Poultry Corp. v. United States, 295 U.S. 495, 541–542 (1935) (emphasis added).

16 William H. Rehnquist, *The Supreme Court: How It Was, How It Is* (New York: Morrow, 1987), 229.

17 Yakus v. United States, 321 U.S. 414, 426 (1944).

18 *Yakus*, 321 U.S. at 451–452.

19 Cynthia R. Farina, "Statutory Interpretation and the Balance of Power in the Administrative State," *Columbia Law Review* 89 (1989): 487 (emphasis in the original).

20 *Industrial Union*, 448 U.S. at 675.

21 *Industrial Union*, 448 U.S. at 687 (emphasis added).

22 Whitman v. American Trucking Associations, Inc., 531 U.S. 457, 465 (2001).

23 *Whitman*, 531 U.S. at 476.

24 Martin H. Redish, *The Constitution as Political Structure* (New York: Oxford University Press, 1995), 136–137 (emphasis added).

25 David Schoenbrod, "The Delegation Doctrine: Could the Court Give It Substance?" *Michigan Law Review* 83 (April 1985): 1254.

26 Gary Lawson, "Delegation and Original Meaning," *Virginia Law Review* 88, no. 2 (2002): 329.

27 Lawson, "Delegation and Original Meaning," 376.

28 *Wayman*, 23 U.S. at 45 (emphasis added).

29 Metzger, "The Supreme Court 2016 Term: 1930s Redux," 7.

30 Metzger, "The Supreme Court 2016 Term: 1930s Redux," 16.

31 Adrian Vermeule, "What Legitimacy Crisis?" Part of "Questioning the Administrative State," *Cato Unbound* (2016), https://www.cato-unbound.org/2016/05/09/adrian-vermeule/what-legitimacy-crisis.

32 Vermeule, "What Legitimacy Crisis?" (emphasis in the original).

33 Vermeule, "What Legitimacy Crisis?"

34 Vermeule, "What Legitimacy Crisis?"
35 S. Rept. 752, 79th Cong., 1st Sess. (1945), https://www.justice.gov/sites/default/files/jmd/legacy/2014/03/20/senaterept-752-1945.pdf.
36 National Broadcasting Co., Inc. v. United States, 319 U.S. 190 (1943).
37 *Whitman*, 531 U.S. at 487.
38 U.S. Department of Transportation v. Association of American Railroads, 135 S. Ct. 1225, 1254 (2015).
39 United States v. Nichols, 784 F.3d at 667 et seq.
40 U.S. Telecom Assoc. v. FCC, slip op., 9 (May 1, 2017) (emphasis in the original).

CHAPTER 7: THE *CHEVRON* DOCTRINE

1 *Chevron*, 467 U.S. at 843.
2 *Chevron*, 467 U.S. at 844.
3 *Chevron*, 467 U.S. at 845 (quoting United States v. Shimer, 367 U.S. 374 at 383 [1961]).
4 *Chevron*, 467 U.S. at 845.
5 *Chevron*, 467 U.S. at 865.
6 *Chevron*, 467 U.S. at 865–866.
7 *Chevron*, 467 U.S. at 866 (quoting *TVA v. Hill*, 437 U.S. 153, 195 [1978]).
8 *Chevron*, 467 U.S. at 845.
9 Hamburger, *Is Administrative Law Unlawful?*, 490.
10 Philip Hamburger, "Gorsuch's Collision Course with the Administrative State," *New York Times* (March 20, 2017).
11 Bowles v. Seminole Rock & Sand Co., 325 U.S. 410, 414 (1945).
12 Auer v. Robbins, 519 U.S. 452, 461 (1997) (quoting *Bowles*, 325 U.S. at 414).
13 *City of Arlington*, 569 U.S. at 296.
14 *City of Arlington*, 569 U.S. at 300.
15 *City of Arlington*, 569 U.S. at 304.
16 *City of Arlington*, 569 U.S. at 312–313 (Roberts dissenting).
17 *City of Arlington*, 569 U.S. at 315.
18 *City of Arlington*, 569 U.S. at 316.
19 *City of Arlington*, 569 U.S. at 318.
20 *City of Arlington*, 569 U.S. at 318.
21 *City of Arlington*, 569 U.S. at 327.
22 Pereira v. Sessions, 585 U.S. _____ (2018).
23 Perez v. Mortgage Bankers Ass'n, 135 S. Ct. 1199, at 1211 (2015).
24 *Perez*, 135 S. Ct. at 1213 (emphasis added) (Thomas concurring).
25 Gutierrez-Brizuela v. Lynch, 834 F.3rd 1142, 1158 (10th Cir., 2016) (emphasis in the original).
26 *Gutierrez-Brizuela*, 834 F.3rd at 1149.
27 The Loan Syndications and Trading Association v. Securities and Exchange Commission and Board of Governors of the Federal Reserve System, Slip Op., February 9, 2018.
28 *Loan Syndications and Trading Association*, 4 (quoting Entergy v. Riverkeeper, 556 U.S. 208 [2009]).
29 Chamber of Commerce of the United States v. U.S. Department of Labor, Slip Op, 5th Cir., March 15, 2018.

30 Farina, "Statutory Interpretation and the Balance of Power in the Administrative State," 525.

31 As discussed earlier, Justice Rehnquist thought that the delegation was so broad as to be unconstitutional under the nondelegation doctrine.

32 See, e.g., Richard B. Stewart, "Reformation of Administrative Law," *Harvard Law Review* 88, no. 8 (1975): 1669–1813.

CONCLUSION

1 See, e.g., the following from Metzger, "The Supreme Court 2016 Term: 1930s Redux," 71–72, notable for its undemonstrated assumptions and circularity about delegations of power: "The administrative state—with its bureaucracy, expert and professional personnel, and internal institutional complexity—performs critical constitutional functions and is the key to an accountable, constrained, and effective executive branch. Indeed, far from being constitutionally suspect, the administrative state today is constitutionally obligatory, rendered necessary by the broad statutory delegations of authority to the executive branch that are the defining feature of modern government. Those delegations are here to stay; only the most extreme and resolute anti-administrativists are willing to suggest their invalidation, and the Supreme Court has almost never done so. From delegation, however, core features of the national administrative state follow."

2 Monmouth University Polling Institute, "Low Public Confidence in the American System" (January 4, 2018), https://www.monmouth.edu/polling-institute/documents/monmouthpoll_us_010418-2.pdf/ (emphasis added). The headline is misleading; it refers to the public's view that the Congress and the president are not working together as they should, and that the Founders would be disappointed.

3 William H. Rehnquist, "The Notion of a Living Constitution," *Harvard Journal of Law and Public Policy* 29, no. 2 (1976): 409.

INDEX

Page numbers followed by *f* or n indicate figures or notes.

House of Representatives. *See* Congress
Housing industry, regulations and
    differences between financial and
    construction sectors, 79–80, 80f
Hovenkamp, Herbert, 58, 64, 66
Hughes, Charles Evans: *A.L.A. Schechter
    Poultry v. United States*, 123; New Deal
    and, xiii, 71, 72; *Panama Refining v.
    Ryan*, 122

Immigration and Nationality Act, 25
Immigration restrictions, in Progressive
    Era, 60
*Industrial Union Department, AFL-CIO v.
    American Petroleum Institute*, 48, 50, 53,
    126–127, 159
Innovation: business's need to recoup costs
    of, 106–107; net neutrality as reducer
    of, 105–107
Intelligible principle concept, Congress's
    delegation of authority, 120–121,
    127–128, 130, 132, 135–136
Internet service providers (ISPs), threat
    of reduced innovation due to net
    neutrality regulations, 105–107
Interstate Commerce Commission (ICC),
    62, 69, 87, 103–104
"Invisible hand," of markets, 78
Ipse dixit character, of legislation, 110
Is Administrative Law Unlawful?
    (Hamburger), 64

Jackson, Robert, 72
Jim Crow laws, Progressives and, 60
Johnson, Boris, xx–xxi
Johnson, Lyndon B., 42
Jones & Laughlin v. NLRB, 124–125
JPMorgan Chase, 87
Judicial restraint, and courts' place in
    structure of Constitution, 24–25, 32–33,
    82–83, 147–150
Judicial review: Administrative Procedure
    Act and, xv, 47, 51–52, 70, 83, 134, 137; as
    caution for Congress, xv, 51–54; *Chevron*
    and, 138, 144–145, 148, 153, 155–157;
    Framers' intentions for, xv–xvi, 16,
    24–25, 53; Marshall and "what the law
    is," xv, xxii, 29, 34, 114, 138–139, 151, 152,
    154–155, 161; Progressives and, 74
Judiciary: failure to rein in administrative
    state, x–xi, xv, xvi, xxii, xiv, 19–20,
    82–83, 134, 136, 146, 161; Framers' intent
    and interpretation of laws, 57–58; role

in separation of powers, 24–25, 28–30,
    33, 109
Judiciary Act (1789), 116
Justice Department, Operation Choke Point
    and, 9–11
J. W. Hampton, Jr. v. United States, 120–121,
    127–128

Kagan, Elena, 112
Kahn, Alfred, 103
Kavanaugh, Brett: *Chevron* and, xxiv–xxv,
    152, 155; *Loan Syndication and Trading
    Association*, 155, 156; net neutrality and,
    136; nondelegation doctrine and, 136
Kennedy, Anthony: *Chevron* and, xxv; *City of
    Arlington v. FCC*, 150; *Pereira v. Sessions*,
    152
Kennedy, John F., 42, 144
Kersch, Ken, 63, 67
Kessler, Gladys, 11
Keynes, John Maynard, 67
Kirzner, Israel M., 85–86
Krugman, Paul, 89–90

La Follette, Robert, 60
Landis, James M., 68
Lawson, Gary, 129–130
Legal scholars, nondelegation doctrine
    and, 128–134; administrative state's
    legislative authority and, 131–134;
    dismissive attitude toward, 130–131;
    economic regulation and, 129–130;
    "goals statutes" and "rules statutes"
    and, 128–129
Legislature: administrative agencies and
    laws not written by, 37–38; Progressives
    and circumventing of popular will, 40,
    59, 61–64; signal role of, xiv, 141; value
    of separating from executive, x, 142, 146,
    161. *See also* Congress; Nondelegation
    doctrine
Legitimacy, and administrative agencies:
    arising from laws made by Congress,
    30, 70; Brexit and voters' understanding
    of, xxii, xxiv, 75, 165; *Chevron* and, 157;
    election of president and administrative
    agencies as part of executive branch,
    xiv–xv, 133; judiciary's constitutional
    role and, 134; lacking in unelected
    bureaucracy, 161–165; moral authority
    and, 75, 165–166; Progressives and,
    70, 75; provided by president, xiv–xv,
    140–143; Vermeule on, 131–133